TEEN RIGHTS AND FREEDOMS

Freedom of Assembly and Association

TEEN RIGHTS AND FREEDOMS

Freedom of Assembly and Association

Noël Merino
Book Editor

GREENHAVEN PRESS
A part of Gale, Cengage Learning

Detroit • New York • San Francisco • New Haven, Conn • Waterville, Maine • London

Elizabeth Des Chenes, *Managing Editor*

© 2012 Greenhaven Press, a part of Gale, Cengage Learning

Gale and Greenhaven Press are registered trademarks used herein under license.

For more information, contact:
Greenhaven Press
27500 Drake Rd.
Farmington Hills, MI 48331-3535
Or you can visit our Internet site at gale.cengage.com.

For product information and technology assistance, contact us at:

Gale Customer Support, 1-800-877-4253.
For permission to use material from this text or product, submit all requests online at www.cengage.com/permissions.

Further permissions questions can be emailed to permissionrequest@cengage.com.

Articles in Greenhaven Press anthologies are often edited for length to meet page requirements. In addition, original titles of these works are changed to clearly present the main thesis and to explicitly indicate the author's opinion. Every effort is made to ensure the Greenhaven Press accurately reflects the original intent of the authors. Every effort has been made to trace the owners of copyrighted material.

Cover Image © Joseph Reid/Alamy.

LIBRARY OF CONGRESS CATALOGING-IN-PUBLICATION DATA

Freedom of assembly and association / Noël Merino, book editor.
    p. cm. -- (Teen rights and freedoms)
    Includes bibliographical references and index.
    ISBN 978-0-7377-5828-3 (hardcover)
    1. Freedom of association--United States. 2. Assembly, Right of--United States.
I. Merino, Noël.
    KF4778.F734 2012
    342.7308'54--dc23
                                            2011041398

Printed in the United States of America
1 2 3 4 5 6 7 16 15 14 13 12

Contents

A director for the National Youth Rights Association (NYRA) argues there is no solid evidence supporting the claim that juvenile curfews reduce crime.

Foreword

> *"In the truest sense freedom cannot be
> bestowed, it must be achieved."*
> Franklin D. Roosevelt,
> September 16, 1936

The notion of children and teens having rights is a relatively recent development. Early in American history, the head of the household—nearly always the father—exercised complete control over the children in the family. Children were legally considered to be the property of their parents. Over time, this view changed, as society began to acknowledge that children have rights independent of their parents, and that the law should protect young people from exploitation. By the early twentieth century, more and more social reformers focused on the welfare of children, and over the ensuing decades advocates worked to protect them from harm in the workplace, to secure public education for all, and to guarantee fair treatment for youths in the criminal justice system. Throughout the twentieth century, rights for children and teens—and restrictions on those rights—were established by Congress and reinforced by the courts. Today's courts are still defining and clarifying the rights and freedoms of young people, sometimes expanding those rights and sometimes limiting them. Some teen rights are outside the scope of public law and remain in the realm of the family, while still others are determined by school policies.

Each volume in the Teen Rights and Freedoms series focuses on a different right or freedom and offers an anthology of key essays and articles on that right or freedom and the responsibilities that come with it. Material within each volume is drawn from a diverse selection of primary and secondary sources—journals, magazines, newspapers, nonfiction books, organization newsletters, position papers, speeches, and government documents, with a particular emphasis on Supreme Court and lower court decisions. Volumes also include first-person narratives from young people and others involved in teen rights issues, such as parents and educators. The material is selected and arranged to highlight all the major social and legal controversies relating to the right or freedom under discussion. Each selection is preceded by an introduction that provides context and background. In many cases, the essays point to the difference between adult and teen rights, and why this difference exists.

Many of the volumes cover rights guaranteed under the Bill of Rights and how these rights are interpreted and protected in regard to children and teens, including freedom of speech, freedom of the press, due process, and religious rights. The scope of the series also encompasses rights or freedoms, whether real or perceived, relating to the school environment, such as electronic devices, dress, Internet policies, and privacy. Some volumes focus on the home environment, including topics such as parental control and sexuality.

Numerous features are included in each volume of Teen Rights and Freedoms:

- An annotated **table of contents** provides a brief summary of each essay in the volume and highlights court decisions and personal narratives.

- An **introduction** specific to the volume topic gives context for the right or freedom and its impact on daily life.

- A brief **chronology** offers important dates associated with the right or freedom, including landmark court cases.

- **Primary sources**—including personal narratives and court decisions—are among the varied selections in the anthology.

- **Illustrations**—including photographs, charts, graphs, tables, statistics, and maps—are closely tied to the text and chosen to help readers understand key points or concepts.

- An annotated list of **organizations to contact** presents sources of additional information on the topic.
- A **for further reading** section offers a bibliography of books, periodical articles, and Internet sources for further research.
- A comprehensive subject **index** provides access to key people, places, events, and subjects cited in the text.

Each volume of Teen Rights and Freedoms delves deeply into the issues most relevant to the lives of teens: their own rights, freedoms, and responsibilities. With the help of this series, students and other readers can explore from many angles the evolution and current expression of rights both historic and contemporary.

Introduction

The First Amendment to the US Constitution states:

> Congress shall make no law respecting an establishment of
> religion, or prohibiting the free exercise thereof; or abridging
> the freedom of speech, or of the press; or the right of the peo-
> ple peaceably to assemble, and to petition the Government for
> a redress of grievances.

The freedom of assembly comes from this explicit statement that government may not prohibit "the right of the people to peaceably assemble." However, the Constitution does not explicitly mention a freedom of association. Freedom of association has been found by the US Supreme Court, however, to be implicitly guaranteed by the Constitution, stemming from the First Amendment freedoms of assembly, speech, press, and petition.

The freedom of assembly, by its very nature, involves more than one individual, and often involves large numbers of individuals assembled together with the goal of expressing political ideas. As noted in the First Amendment, freedom of assembly extends only to assembly that is done "peaceably." This limit has been interpreted by the Supreme Court to allow the restriction of assembly that is violent, impinges on private property, or otherwise affects the peaceful running of society, such as stopping traffic or placing burdens on public authorities. This does not mean assemblies that disrupt the normal running of society can be prohibited altogether, but government may require that permits be acquired for assemblies that need extra law enforcement or will disrupt traffic, for instance. Unlawful assemblies, with intent to break the law, may be prohibited. Furthermore, whereas assemblies in public squares or public streets are usually protected, assemblies on private property may be more tightly regulated, if not prohibited altogether.

The freedom of association is very closely linked with the freedom of assembly. Whereas the freedom of assembly involves the right to physically assemble with other people, the freedom of association goes beyond mere physical assembly to protect the right to associate with political groups and other unions. The Court has recognized two distinct kinds of constitutionally protected association: expressive association and intimate association. The right to expressive association protects the right to engage in group activities that have an expressive element, either through speech, writing, or assembly. The right to intimate association protects the right to maintain intimate human relationships and has been recognized by the Court in matters of marriage, reproduction, and sexual relations.

Regarding the freedom of assembly, the key issues to come before the Supreme Court involve restrictions on the time, place, and manner of assemblies. The Supreme Court has a long history of protecting the freedom of assembly, starting in 1939 when in *Hague v. C.I.O.* the Court held that peaceful demonstrators in public forums such as those in streets and parks may not be prosecuted for disorderly conduct. In the 1963 case of *Edwards v. South Carolina* the Court ruled that the state acted unconstitutionally when it ordered students who peacefully assembled on government grounds to leave. In general, the Court has protected the rights of both teens and adults to assemble in public, albeit allowing reasonable restrictions by local governments on the time, place, and manner of assembly. One area where courts have treated teens differently than adults is with respect to juvenile curfews, which restrict the presence of juveniles in public— assembled or not—at certain times of day. The Supreme Court has not addressed this issue yet, and lower courts have differed on their opinions on whether curfew laws unduly restrict the associational rights of minors.

The Supreme Court began protecting the freedom of association in the middle of the twentieth century. In *National Association for the Advancement of Colored People (NAACP) v.*

Alabama (1958), the Court not only ruled that the Constitution protected the right to freely associate in a membership group, but it also ruled that such association has privacy protections, determining that Alabama officials could not demand a list of members of the NAACP. The Court has not always protected student associations: In *Waugh v. Board of Trustees of the University of Mississippi* (1915) the Court said that it was constitutional for public schools to prohibit fraternities in order to protect students from distraction. And, although in *Healy v. James* (1972), the Court determined that schools may not deny certain student groups school privileges due to disapproval, it did note that schools have more latitude than other authorities for limiting certain associations.

The Court first recognized the freedom of intimate association in *Griswold v. Connecticut* (1965), arguing that the right to association and the right to privacy protect married people from laws outlawing contraceptive use. The Court later extended this particular right of intimate association to unmarried people, including minors in *Carey v. Population Services International* (1977).

The constitutionally guaranteed freedom of assembly and freedom of association are important rights for both teens and adults. These freedoms protect activity as varied as political demonstrations, club membership, and access to contraception. The key court cases involving teen assembly and expression, and commentary on these rights, are explored in *Teen Rights and Freedoms: Freedom of Assembly and Association*.

Chronology

1791
The Bill of Rights is adopted by the United States, of which the First Amendment reads: "Congress shall make no law respecting an establishment of religion, or prohibiting the free exercise thereof; or abridging the freedom of speech, or of the press; or the right of the people peaceably to assemble, and to petition the Government for a redress of grievances."

1876
In *United States v. Cruikshank* the Supreme Court first explicitly mentions the right to freedom of assembly as "an attribute of national citizenship" that may not be limited by actions of the federal government.

1915
In *Waugh v. Board of Trustees of the University of Mississippi* the Supreme Court upholds as constitutional a Mississippi statute prohibiting fraternities and other secret societies in all public educational institutions in order to save students from harmful distraction.

1928
In *Bryant v. Zimmerman* the Supreme Court upholds as compatible with freedom of assembly a state statute aimed at the Ku Klux Klan, which required secret organizations with more than twenty people to supply a list of members.

1937
In *DeJonge v. Oregon* the Supreme Court rules that the right of peaceable assembly may not be restricted by state governments, placing the right on the same level as freedom of speech and freedom of the press, guaranteed by the federal government.

1939
In *Hague v. C.I.O.* the Supreme Court determines that peaceful demonstrators in public forums, such as those in streets and parks, may not be prosecuted for disorderly conduct.

1958
In *National Association for the Advancement of Colored People (NAACP) v. Alabama* the Supreme Court makes its first recognition of a right to freedom of association, ruling that from freedom of assembly comes a broader freedom of association, including privacy protections to protect the freedom.

1960
In *Shelton v. Tucker* the Supreme Court rules that an Arkansas law requiring teachers to disclose organizational affiliation violates a teacher's right of free association.

1963
In *Edwards v. South Carolina* the Supreme Court rules that South Carolina violated the rights of freedom of speech, freedom of assembly, and freedom to petition of students who

peacefully assembled on government grounds and were ordered to disperse.

1965   In *Griswold v. Connecticut* the Supreme Court first recognizes a right of freedom of intimate association, finding a state law prohibiting the use of contraceptives unconstitutional.

1972   In *Healy v. James* the Supreme Court rules that it is a violation of the right of student association to be denied university recognition because of disapproval of the group.

1977   In *Carey v. Population Services International* the Supreme Court rules that the rights to privacy and intimate association identified in *Griswold v. Connecticut* (1965) also extend to minors.

1984   In *Roberts v. United States Jaycees* the Supreme Court determines that the policy of the United States Jaycees, a civic and service association, of excluding women was not protected by freedom of association due to its discriminatory nature.

1989   In *City of Dallas v. Stanglin* the Supreme Court rules that a Texas law setting an age restriction in dance halls does not violate the First Amendment associational rights of minors.

1990

In *Board of Education of Westside Community Schools v. Mergens* the Supreme Court rules that public high schools must allow religious groups to meet on campus as long as the schools allow non-curricular clubs in general.

1993

In *Qutb v. Strauss* the US Court of the Appeals for the Fifth Circuit holds that children's and parents' rights are not violated by a juvenile curfew ordinance aimed at protecting young people.

1995

In *Hurley v. Irish-American Gay, Lesbian, and Bisexual Group of Boston* the Supreme Court rules that private organizations, in this case the South Boston Allied War Veterans Council, may exclude groups from a public demonstration without being unlawfully discriminatory.

1997

In *Nunez v. City of San Diego* the US Court of Appeals for the Ninth Circuit holds that a juvenile curfew law violated the rights of minors by not being narrowly tailored enough to achieve its goal.

1998

In *Schleifer v. City of Charlottesville* the US Court of Appeals for the Fourth Circuit upholds a juvenile curfew law noting that the liberty rights of minors are less fundamental than those of adults.

1999

In *Hutchins v. District of Columbia* the DC Circuit Court rules that government interest in protecting the welfare of minors justifies the limitation of their rights through a juvenile curfew law.

2000

In *Boy Scouts of America v. Dale* the Supreme Court rules that the Boy Scouts has a right to express its association's identity by rejecting leaders who publicly accept the legitimacy of homosexual conduct.

2007

In *Chi Iota Colony of Alpha Epsilon Pi Fraternity v. City University of New York* the US Court of Appeals for the Second District rules that a university's non-discrimination policy did not violate the freedom of association rights of members in an all-male fraternity.

> "Without the freedom to assemble, the
> right to associate, and the liberty to
> project speech through group activism,
> free expression would be a solitary and
> stifled guarantee indeed."

The Freedom of Assembly Supports the Freedom of Association

Adam Newton

In the following viewpoint Adam Newton contends that the freedom of assembly guaranteed by the First Amendment to the US Constitution is an important right necessary to support freedom of group speech. Newton illustrates how the US Supreme Court has come to identify a freedom of association, even though such a right is not explicitly mentioned in the Constitution. Associational rights stem from the right to assemble, among other constitutional rights, the author claims. Newton explains how associational rights have been understood by the courts with respect to juvenile curfew laws, the right to expressive association, and the right to political association; and how government can limit the right to association. Newton is counsel in the legal division at Procter & Gamble headquarters in Cincinnati.

The freedom of assembly is one of the few constitutional liberties that the Framers graced with an adverb, securing the right of the people "peaceably to assemble." Were the freedom of assembly limited to orderly gatherings in public parks, however, exercise of this right would implicate only clean streets and crowd control. But ideas, and the rights that protect them, are far more important.

The civil rights era in this country prompted the Supreme Court to consider the collective beliefs that animate crowds and the voice—be it roar or oration—with which the group speaks. This emphasis on a conceptual in addition to a corporeal right to meet and discuss ideas led to the recognition of a right of association. As the Supreme Court observed in 1958, "It is beyond debate that freedom to engage in association for the advancement of beliefs and ideas is an inseparable aspect of the 'liberty' assured by the Due Process Clause of the Fourteenth Amendment, which embraces freedom of speech."

Though the Constitution does not expressly set forth a freedom of association, at least three strands of law intersect at the junction of group speech: the right of assembly, the privacy of intimate bonds, and freedom of expression. Appropriately, the association doctrine reflects its subject: Constitutional protection for the group involves diverse principles speaking in chorus.

Balancing Associational Interests

Because assembly involves free expression, the congregational aspects of this First Amendment guarantee fit neatly in the "time, place, and manner" doctrine set forth in *United States v. O'Brien* (1968). As long as people "peaceably" convene to picket, protest, or distribute handbills, the state may not penalize the assembly. However, this protection does not immunize the gathering from generally applicable health, safety and welfare laws designed to protect private property, eliminate litter, curb visual blight, facilitate traffic, control noise or minimize congestion.

Though the time-place-manner concept may be easily articulated, associational interests still present challenges when the doctrine is applied. Courts must examine the government's justification to ensure that the challenged regulation is indeed indifferent to the content of the speech. The scope of that inquiry depends on where the assembly takes place. Courts will strictly scrutinize regulations that attempt to limit assembly in places traditionally open to the public such as parks or sidewalks. Strict scrutiny is the highest level of review and requires the government to show that the ordinance is narrowly tailored to achieve a compelling government interest. License or permit requirements that favor or discourage certain groups, or that vest total discretion in officials to grant such permits, are usually struck down.

Shuttlesworth v. Birmingham (1969), for instance, struck down a parade ordinance that "conferred upon the City Commission virtually unbridled and absolute power to prohibit any 'parade,' 'procession,' or 'demonstration' on the city's streets or public ways."

Procedural safeguards must protect the rights of all speakers or none—even members of the Nazi party who intend to march through a predominantly Jewish section of an Illinois city—as the 1977 U.S. Supreme Court ruled in *National Socialist Party v. Skokie*. The fact-sensitive balancing between regulators and those who assemble requires careful line-drawing—sometimes literally. In cases concerning anti-abortion protests, for example, restrictions have been allowed to keep protesters a certain distance away from women approaching abortion clinics.

Juvenile Curfew Laws

Particularly suspect are blanket regulations that upset the balance *O'Brien* strikes between the government interest asserted and the incidental burden on First Amendment rights. In *City of Chicago v. Morales*, for example, the Supreme Court in 1999 struck down a municipal code that criminalized loitering, which was defined as "to remain in any one place with no apparent

FIRST AMENDMENT RIGHTS ARE NOT WIDELY KNOWN

Freedom of the press	17%
Freedom of speech	62%
Freedom of religion	19%
Right to petition	3%
Right of assembly	14%
Don't know	30%

Taken from: First Amendment Center, "State of the First Amendment," July 2011.

purpose." Though the law was enacted to fight gang activity, it improperly penalized much harmless activity and granted officers immense discretion in assessing which kinds of behavior violated the ordinance. Similarly, juvenile curfew laws have been challenged for trampling on the rights of minors to meet and gather. Such ordinances have survived only because they exempt activities protected under the First Amendment.

In 1993, the 5th U.S. Circuit Court of Appeals ruled in favor of a Dallas curfew ordinance in *Qutb v. Strauss.* The 5th Circuit examined the ordinance under strict-scrutiny review and upheld it. The court concluded that the city, by including exceptions to the ordinance, most notably exceptions for minors exercising their First Amendment rights, had enacted a narrowly drawn ordinance that respected the rights of juveniles and allowed the city to meet its goal of increasing juvenile safety and decreasing juvenile crime.

The Dallas ordinance became the model for cities around the country wishing to enact curfew ordinances. The 9th Circuit underscored the importance of the exceptions when, in its 1997 ruling *Nunez v. San Diego*, it declared a San Diego curfew ordinance unconstitutional. The 9th Circuit ruled, in part, that the ordinance was not narrowly tailored to minimize burdens on fundamental rights. The court, in particular, noted that "San Diego rejected a proposal to tailor the ordinance more narrowly by adopting the broader exceptions used in the ordinance upheld in *Qutb*."

However, there is quite a difference of opinion among various courts as to what standard applies when analyzing curfew statutes. Some, including the 5th and 9th Circuits and the Florida Supreme Court, use strict scrutiny because fundamental rights such as speech and assembly are implicated, as well as the right to freedom of movement. Although other courts may agree that fundamental rights are implicated, they have a different opinion as to the status of minors.

The Rights of Minors

The U.S. Supreme Court has recognized that the rights of minors are not as wide-ranging as those of adults. Minors enjoy the same constitutional protections as adults, but due to "their unique vulnerability, immaturity, and need for parental guidance," the state is within its bounds to exercise greater control over their activities. Following this rationale, many courts, including the 2nd, 4th, 7th and D.C. Circuits, have used intermediate scrutiny to review curfew laws. Intermediate scrutiny requires the government to show that a law is substantially related to an important government interest.

Due to the inconsistencies and disagreements within the courts, the standards for what is an acceptable curfew law and what is unacceptable are not clear. While some of the ordinances modeled after the Dallas law survived constitutional challenges, not all did.

In June 2003, the 2nd Circuit declared a curfew ordinance in Vernon, Conn., unconstitutional because it infringed on the rights of minors under the 14th Amendment's equal-protection clause. In this particular case, the writing of the ordinance and the exceptions it contained were not the issue, rather it was the necessity of the ordinance. The town of Vernon passed the ordinance to reduce juvenile crime and victimization at night but, according to the court, failed to provide the requisite proof that the ordinance was needed. Since the curfew restricted constitutional rights of juveniles, the town had to show that the ordinance was substantially related to an important government interest. While all parties agreed with the aims of the ordinance, the town failed to show that juvenile crime was a problem during the curfew hours, thus the 2nd Circuit found in *Ramos v. Town of Vernon* that the ordinance was not substantially related to the town's interest in preventing juvenile crime.

In January 2004 another curfew ordinance fell when the 7th Circuit declared an Indianapolis law unconstitutional. Indianapolis amended its curfew ordinance in 2001 to include exceptions for the exercise of First Amendment rights. The 7th Circuit, however, found that the First Amendment defense provided in the statute was inadequate since it did not require a law enforcement official to look into whether any exceptions included in the statute applied before making an arrest. So, if an officer came across a juvenile walking down the street returning from a late night protest, the officer could arrest him without even inquiring into why he was out. The court ruled in *Hodgkins v. Peterson* that the possibility of arrest was intimidating enough to chill a juvenile's exercise of his First Amendment rights.

Image on Following Page: Students and NAACP members march in Washington, DC, on May 25, 1979. In 1958 the Supreme Court ruled that states could not force the NAACP to disclose its membership list. © Pictorial Parade/Hulton Archive/Getty Images.

Two curfew ordinances were thrown out by the Florida Supreme Court in November 2004. This case consolidated challenges to ordinances in Tampa and Pinellas Park. In *Florida v. J.P.*, the court used strict-scrutiny analysis when looking at the laws and found that neither [was] "narrowly tailored" and the criminal penalties both ordinances called for were contrary to the stated purpose of protecting minors from victimization.

Many cities enact curfews with the hope that they will prevent minors from committing, or being the victim of, late night crime. Opponents challenge curfew ordinances citing the restriction of minors' First Amendment rights. Although curfews do affect these rights, such as the right to associate with friends, courts have found these restrictions can be justified if the city proves the need for such a law.

The Right to Expressive Association

The right to free association extends beyond intimate relationships. Groups peaceably joined to engage in First Amendment activities also enjoy protection from government interference. To constitute "expressive association," such interaction must be defined by common political, cultural or economic activism. Social gatherings that are intended for leisure and diversion do not qualify and may be regulated by the government for any rational purpose. For instance, in the 1989 case *City of Dallas v. Stanglin*, the Supreme Court upheld a local ordinance limiting use of dance halls to teens between ages 14 and 18.

When people in an expressive association object to government action on First Amendment grounds, courts consider the extent to which the challenged regulation or statute interferes with the advocacy of the group. In *NAACP v. Alabama* (1958), the Court concluded that the state could not compel disclosure of the group's membership list under a statute that required such information from out-of-state corporations. In the tumultuous civil rights era, the Court recognized that divulging the names of NAACP [National Association for the Advancement of Colored

People] members would expose them to attack and so undermine the ability of the group to advocate its message.

For some expressive groups, the membership *is* the message. Generally applicable public-accommodation laws designed to foster inclusiveness can have the effect of forced speech in derogation of an organization's principles. In *Boy Scouts of America v. Dale*, the Court in 2000 agreed with the scouting organization that inclusion of an openly gay scoutmaster—otherwise required under New Jersey's public-accommodation law—would unconstitutionally undermine the organization's promotion of "morally straight and clean values" in youth.

Likewise, in *Hurley v. Irish-American Gay, Lesbian & Bisexual Group*, the 1995 Court held that a state public-accommodation law could not require the South Boston Allied War Veterans' Council to include gay marchers in its St. Patrick's Day parade. According to the Court, application of this law would interfere with the group's social and religious agenda and violate its First Amendment rights as parade sponsor.

In such cases, the Court examines the tradition, practices and selection criteria of the group to determine if these cohere into shared speech. If so, the Court will then assess whether state regulation of the internal organization and affairs of the group would impair the group's common expression. In *Roberts v. United States Jaycees*, the Supreme Court determined in 1984 that Minnesota's interest in outlawing gender discrimination would not significantly undermine the educational and charitable mission of the historically all-male organization. Thus, the state could constitutionally require the group to admit women as full members. The Court reached the same result in applying the California Unruh [Civil Rights] Act against the Rotary Club, concluding that inclusion of women would not require the all-male members to "abandon their basic goals of humanitarian service, high ethical standards in all vocations, good will, and peace" (*Board of Directors of Rotary International v. Rotary Club of Duarte*, 1987).

The Right to Political Association

A different problem arises when the government seeks to punish or reward public employees based on their group affiliations. To condition a benefit—the employment contract—on a state employee's participation in or disavowal of a certain political party violates the First Amendment. In *Rutan v. Republican Party of Illinois* (1990) the Court extended this prohibition to promotions, transfers and recalls of government employees on the basis of patronage. The only exception is for government workers who hold policy-level or confidential positions.

The state may, however, require public employees to declare an oath affirming allegiance to the constitutional processes of government. Negative oaths that disavow past conduct or belief are constitutional only to the extent that the activity disclaimed could have resulted in the denial of public employment, such as knowing advocacy of the violent overthrow of the United States. Public employees and others subject to state regulation also have a right *not* to associate. Thus, lawyers subject to mandatory bar fees and workers who pay required union dues may not be compelled to finance political and ideological causes they oppose. Though the conduct described here involves speech, it could be termed associational speech—in that conditioning public benefits (a job) on an oath concerning whether a person does or does not belong or harbor loyalty to certain groups implicates the right to join or not join these causes.

Citizens who wish to oppose Democrats and Republicans alike have a right, under their freedom of association, "to create and develop new political parties," the Supreme Court said in the 1992 case *Norman v. Reed*. However, this freedom is checked by the state's interest in preventing voter confusion, promoting legitimate competition in light of limited ballot space, preventing ballot manipulation, and discouraging party splintering. In balancing the need for an orderly election process against the citizens' right to associate in political parties of their choosing, the Court weighs the "character and magnitude" of the burden on associational interests against the state interest in imposing that burden. In *Timmons v. Twin Cities Area New Party* (1997), that balance tilted in favor of the state. Upholding Minnesota's "anti-fusion" laws that prohibited candidates from representing multiple parties on the ballot, the Court held that the need for ballot integrity and stability outweighed the burden on candidates aspiring to multiparty nomination.

When Extremists Assemble

Advanced technology allows like-minded believers to share ideas, distribute messages cheaply and pervasively, and coordinate public campaigns. This trend promises an upcoming test between gatherings of fringe groups and the need for a secure, democratic society. The impulse to suppress unpopular and unsavory messages confirms the importance of the First Amendment to organizations with views to which many people object. The Boy Scouts [is] perhaps the most benign example of such a group.

Certainly, the state may intervene if alarming messages would incite violent or lawless action. But as to the functioning of groups—their membership and internal affairs—*Boy Scouts of America v. Dale* suggests that the state may not impose even generally applicable, otherwise neutral laws that could impair the group's freedom of expression. Doing so not only might frustrate state regulators and law enforcement officials, turning radical groups into impenetrable "black boxes," but would also appear inconsistent with the Supreme Court's free-exercise jurisprudence, which does not exempt religious groups from the effect of neutral, generally applicable laws. The Court will be faced with a difficult decision when, for example, a condominium association claims that its common purpose and continuing mission are to keep the races apart and that, under *Dale*, the state may not force it to accept minority residents.

Should discrimination be any more tolerated simply because it is genuinely believed and consistently shared within a group?

The Right to Peaceful Demonstration

When messages of opposition turn to acts of violence and law-lessness, the Court has required "precision of regulation" before individual members may be held liable by the fact of their belonging. On Oct. 31, 1969, the NAACP coordinated an economic boycott against white businesses in Port Gibson, Miss., after negotiations for racial equality broke down. Though the marches were generally peaceful and orderly, some individuals enforced the boycott through violence and threats of violence. When suit was brought, the Mississippi Supreme Court imposed liability against the entire organization for the lawless acts of certain members. Reversing this ruling, the U.S. Supreme Court said uncontrolled violence by a few members could not be imputed to the group as a whole, which retained constitutional protection for its peaceful demonstration.

As the Court noted:

> Civil liability may not be imposed merely because an individual belonged to a group, some members of which committed acts of violence. For liability to be imposed by reason of association alone, it is necessary to establish that the group itself possessed unlawful goals and that the individual held a specific intent to further those illegal goals.

Fast-forward more than 30 years to when pro-life protesters co-ordinate national demonstrations at abortion clinics. Some members engage in violence, trespass and destruction of private property. The National Organization for Women wins a unanimous jury verdict against prominent pro-life groups under RICO—the Racketeering-Influenced and Corrupt Organization statute, a federal law designed to prosecute organized crime. However, the U.S. Supreme Court dealt a setback to abortion clinics in 2006 in its 8-0 decision in *Scheidler v. National Organization for Women Inc.*, ending the two-decade-old legal fight over anti-abortion protests by ruling that federal extortion and racketeering laws cannot be used to ban demonstrations.

In his book *Democracy in America*, Alexis de Tocqueville noted of his visit to the United States in the 1830s:

> Americans of all ages, all stations in life, and all types of dispositions are forever forming associations. . . . Nothing, in my view, more deserves attention than the intellectual and moral associations in America.

Associations in this country have powerful voices for enduring change: They have ended segregation, ensured fair working conditions, stopped and started wars, protected the environment, and sparked a host of other political, economic and cultural transformations. Without the freedom to assemble, the right to associate, and the liberty to project speech through group activism, free expression would be a solitary and stifled guarantee indeed.

"*South Carolina infringed the petitioners' constitutionally protected rights of free speech, free assembly, and freedom to petition for redress of their grievances.*"

It Is a Violation of Freedom of Assembly to Arrest Peaceful Protestors

The Supreme Court's Decision

Potter Stewart

In the following viewpoint Potter Stewart, writing for the majority of the US Supreme Court, held that the arrest, conviction, and punishment of a group of high school and college students who were peacefully assembled in protest violated the First Amendment. Stewart argued that peaceful demonstration by students is protected by their First Amendment rights of free speech, free assembly, and freedom to petition the government for redress of their grievances. Stewart contends that the state has a right to regulate public assembly in order to protect from disorder. However, he concludes that the Fourteenth Amendment does not allow states to violate the First Amendment rights of citizens to express their views in public simply because such views are unpopular. Stewart was an associate justice of the US Supreme Court from 1958 until 1981.

L ate in the morning of March 2, 1961, the petitioners, high school and college students of the Negro race, met at the Zion Baptist Church in Columbia. From there, at about noon, they walked in separate groups of about 15 to the South Carolina State House grounds, an area of two city blocks open to the general public. Their purpose was

> to submit a protest to the citizens of South Carolina, along with the Legislative Bodies of South Carolina, our feelings and our dissatisfaction with the present condition of discriminatory actions against Negroes in general, and to let them know that we were dissatisfied, and that we would like for the laws which prohibited Negro privileges in this State to be removed.

Already on the State House grounds when the petitioners arrived were 30 or more law enforcement officers, who had advance knowledge that the petitioners were coming. Each group of petitioners entered the grounds through a driveway and parking area known in the record as the "horseshoe." As they entered, they were told by the law enforcement officials that "they had a right, as a citizen, to go through the State House grounds, as any other citizen has, as long as they were peaceful." During the next half hour or 45 minutes, the petitioners, in the same small groups, walked single file or two abreast in an orderly way, through the grounds, each group carrying placards bearing such messages as "I am proud to be a Negro" and "Down with segregation."

Alleged Breach of the Peace

During this time, a crowd of some 200 to 300 onlookers had collected in the horseshoe area and on the adjacent sidewalks. There was no evidence to suggest that these onlookers were anything but curious, and no evidence at all of any threatening remarks, hostile gestures, or offensive language on the part of any member

Students march in peaceful protest to the capitol building in Montgomery, Alabama, in 1960. The Supreme Court ruled in 1963 that the arrest of peaceful protestors in Columbia, South Carolina, violated their First Amendment rights. © Donald Uhrbrock/Time & Life Pictures/ Getty Images.

of the crowd. The City Manager testified that he recognized some of the onlookers, whom he did not identify, as "possible trouble-makers," but his subsequent testimony made clear that nobody among the crowd actually caused or threatened any trouble. There was no obstruction of pedestrian or vehicular traffic within the State House grounds. No vehicle was prevented from enter-ing or leaving the horseshoe area. Although vehicular traffic at a nearby street intersection was slowed down somewhat, an officer was dispatched to keep traffic moving. There were a number of bystanders on the public sidewalks adjacent to the State House grounds, but they all moved on when asked to do so, and there was no impediment of pedestrian traffic. Police protection at the scene was at all times sufficient to meet any foreseeable possibil-ity of disorder.

In the situation and under the circumstances thus described, the police authorities advised the petitioners that they would be arrested if they did not disperse within 15 minutes. Instead of dispersing, the petitioners engaged in what the City Manager described as "boisterous," "loud," and "flamboyant" conduct, which, as his later testimony made clear, consisted of listening to a "religious harangue" by one of their leaders, and loudly sing-ing "The Star Spangled Banner" and other patriotic and religious songs, while stamping their feet and clapping their hands. After 15 minutes had passed, the police arrested the petitioners and marched them off to jail.

Upon this evidence, the state trial court convicted the peti-tioners of breach of the peace, and imposed sentences ranging from a $10 fine or five days in jail to a $100 fine or 30 days in jail. In affirming the judgments, the Supreme Court of South Carolina said that, under the law of that State, the offense of breach of the peace "is not susceptible of exact definition," but that the "general definition of the offense" is as follows:

> In general terms, a breach of the peace is a violation of pub-lic order, a disturbance of the public tranquility, by any act or

conduct inciting to violence . . . it includes any violation of any law enacted to preserve peace and good order. It may consist of an act of violence or an act likely to produce violence. It is not necessary that the peace be actually broken to lay the foundation for a prosecution for this offense. If what is done is unjustifiable and unlawful, tending with sufficient directness to break the peace, no more is required. Nor is actual personal violence an essential element in the offense. . . .

By "peace," as used in the law in this connection, is meant the tranquility enjoyed by citizens of a municipality or community where good order reigns among its members, which is the natural right of all persons in political society.

Basic Constitutional Rights

The petitioners contend that there was a complete absence of any evidence of the commission of this offense, and that they were thus denied one of the most basic elements of due process of law. Whatever the merits of this contention, we need not pass upon it in the present case. The state courts have held that the petitioners' conduct constituted breach of the peace under state law, and we may accept their decision as binding upon us to that extent. But it nevertheless remains our duty in a case such as this to make an independent examination of the whole record. And it is clear to us that, in arresting, convicting, and punishing the petitioners under the circumstances disclosed by this record, South Carolina infringed the petitioners' constitutionally protected rights of free speech, free assembly, and freedom to petition for redress of their grievances.

It has long been established that these First Amendment freedoms are protected by the Fourteenth Amendment from invasion by the States. The circumstances in this case reflect an exercise of these basic constitutional rights in their most pristine and classic form. The petitioners felt aggrieved by laws of South Carolina which allegedly "prohibited Negro privileges in this State." They peaceably assembled at the site of the State

Government, and there peaceably expressed their grievances "to the citizens of South Carolina, along with the Legislative Bodies of South Carolina." Not until they were told by police officials that they must disperse on pain of arrest did they do more. Even then, they but sang patriotic and religious songs after one of their leaders had delivered a "religious harangue." There was no violence or threat of violence on their part, or on the part of any member of the crowd watching them. Police protection was "ample."

This, therefore, was a far cry from the situation in *Feiner v. New York* [1951], where two policemen were faced with a crowd which was "pushing, shoving and milling around," where at least one member of the crowd "threatened violence if the police did not act," where "the crowd was pressing closer around petitioner and the officer," and where "the speaker passes the bounds of argument or persuasion and undertakes incitement to riot." And the record is barren of any evidence of "fighting words" [*Chaplinsky v. New Hampshire* (1942)].

The Protection of Unpopular Views

We do not review in this case criminal convictions resulting from the evenhanded application of a precise and narrowly drawn regulatory statute evincing a legislative judgment that certain specific conduct be limited or proscribed. If, for example, the petitioners had been convicted upon evidence that they had violated a law regulating traffic, or had disobeyed a law reasonably limiting the periods during which the State House grounds were open to the public, this would be a different case. These petitioners were convicted of an offense so generalized as to be, in the words of the South Carolina Supreme Court, "not susceptible of exact definition." And they were convicted upon evidence which showed no more than that the opinions which they were peaceably expressing were sufficiently opposed to the views of the majority of the community to attract a crowd and necessitate police protection.

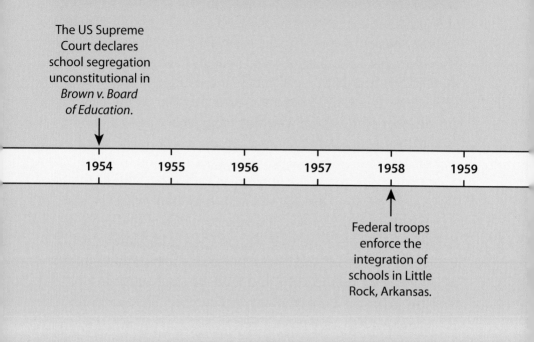

TIMELINE OF KEY CIVIL RIGHTS EVENTS FOR STUDENTS

The US Supreme Court declares school segregation unconstitutional in *Brown v. Board of Education.*

1954 1955 1956 1957 1958 1959

Federal troops enforce the integration of schools in Little Rock, Arkansas.

The Fourteenth Amendment does not permit a State to make criminal the peaceful expression of unpopular views.

[A] function of free speech under our system of government is to invite dispute. It may indeed best serve its high purpose when it induces a condition of unrest, creates dissatisfaction with conditions as they are, or even stirs people to anger. Speech is often provocative and challenging. It may strike at prejudices and preconceptions, and have profound unsettling effects as it presses for acceptance of an idea. That is why freedom of speech . . . is . . . protected against censorship or punishment, unless shown likely to produce a clear and present danger of a serious substantive evil that rises far above public inconvenience, annoyance, or unrest. . . . There is no room

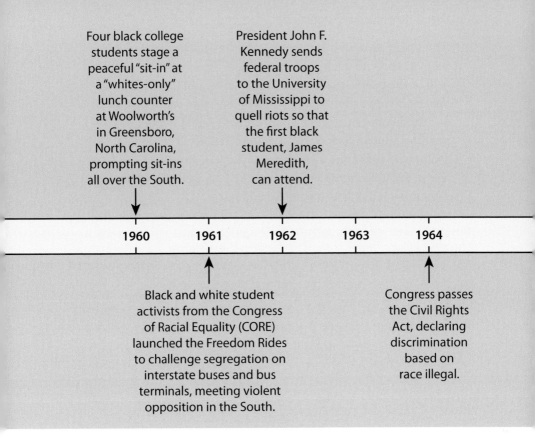

Four black college students stage a peaceful "sit-in" at a "whites-only" lunch counter at Woolworth's in Greensboro, North Carolina, prompting sit-ins all over the South.

President John F. Kennedy sends federal troops to the University of Mississippi to quell riots so that the first black student, James Meredith, can attend.

| 1960 | 1961 | 1962 | 1963 | 1964 |

Black and white student activists from the Congress of Racial Equality (CORE) launched the Freedom Rides to challenge segregation on interstate buses and bus terminals, meeting violent opposition in the South.

Congress passes the Civil Rights Act, declaring discrimination based on race illegal.

under our Constitution for a more restrictive view. For the alternative would lead to standardization of ideas either by legislatures, courts, or dominant political or community groups [*Terminiello v. Chicago* (1949)].

As in the *Terminiello* case, the courts of South Carolina have defined a criminal offense so as to permit conviction of the petitioners if their speech

stirred people to anger, invited public dispute, or brought about a condition of unrest. A conviction resting on any of those grounds may not stand.

As Chief Justice Hughes wrote in *Stromberg v. California* [(1931) :]

The maintenance of the opportunity for free political discussion to the end that government may be responsive to the will of the people and that changes may be obtained by lawful means, an opportunity essential to the security of the Republic, is a fundamental principle of our constitutional system. A statute which, upon its face and as authoritatively construed, is so vague and indefinite as to permit the punishment of the fair use of this opportunity is repugnant to the guaranty of liberty contained in the Fourteenth Amendment. . . .

For these reasons, we conclude that these criminal convictions cannot stand.

VIEWPOINT 3

> "I realized that I could call attention to
> the irony of this situation, the freedom
> to assemble, in a manner a student
> could never hope to accomplish."

A Teacher Stands Up for the Freedom to Assemble

Personal Narrative

Doug Knick

In the following viewpoint Doug Knick recounts his decision to stand in solidarity with a high school student of his who refused to attend a school assembly. Knick explains how his student was given detention for failing to attend a pep rally at school. Knick suggests that if the constitutional freedom to assemble means anything, it must also support the freedom to not assemble by being able to opt out of a school pep rally. Knick explains how he opted to attend detention with the student to show his opposition to the school administration's decision and his support for the student's right to not assemble. Knick, a former high school teacher, is a professor of education at Luther College.

On Thursday afternoon from 3:00 to 4:00 P.M. I served my first high school detention. It only took 46 years for me to reach this milestone. If you are wondering how this is possible, you are correct in concluding that I am not a high school student. I am a high school social studies teacher, a part-time college professor, and a full-time student advocate. The events which led to my self-imposed detention began on Tuesday, November 11, [Veterans] Day [2003].

The Freedom Not to Assemble

Minutes before the student body was to be dismissed from classes in order to assemble in the gymnasium for the traditional flag waving, chest pounding, patriotic pep rally, a young man approached and asked if he had to attend the assembly. The student's request did not come as a surprise [because] on numerous occasions he [had] expressed his struggle with mandated patriotism. I informed the [gentleman] that he had the freedom not to attend the program and since our school has the policy of providing a room for those who elect not to attend lyceums, he should ask the principal where to report. Having similar reservations as this young man, I elected not to attend the ceremony and therefore remained in the classroom.

With the hallway void of bustling students, it was easy to detect the sound of footsteps as they turned the corner and proceeded down the long corridor. As the sneaker clad feet reached the entrance of the classroom silence again filled the hallway. Pulling my eyes from the pages of Scott Hunt's *The Future of Peace* I saw the young man standing in the doorway. Initially, I assumed that the principal instructed the student to return to the classroom, but his face absent of color told me otherwise. Quickly he spewed forth his conversation with the principal and how he did not have the freedom not to attend the Veterans Day program. The administration stated that this was an educational event and attendance was mandatory. When he inquired why, he was instructed that he needed to learn about those who died for his freedom, plus, if he did not attend he would receive detention. The young man now wanted to know, could the administration do that? Could they give him detention?

During our ensuing conversation I challenged the young patriot seated before me to reframe his question. Possibly the issue was not could they, of course they could and WILL, but does that make it right? Together we pondered what freedom means, what it means to be a citizen, and finally a member of the human race. Our conversation was brief and filled with more questions than answers. Closure occurred when the young man informed me that he was going to spend his time reading some articles I had made available on the topic of white privilege.

A Detention of Solidarity

Wednesday when the young man entered the classroom, knowing he would never complain about receiving the detention, I inquired if he indeed was being punished for not attending the program. He shared that he was and that he had been dismissed from the office when he attempted to discuss the issue. I was not surprised by the administration's behavior, this was the same administration which weeks earlier informed me that I was wasting the administration's time by having students identify injustices and develop a plan of action to address the injustice based on Thoreau's "Civil Disobedience." At the end of the class period I informed the student that I would also be serving detention with him.

It needs to be stated clearly, my detention, unlike this student's, was self-imposed. No one was punishing me for not attending the program. I elected to serve the hour of detention and I could do this because I was in a position of power. This position of power was part of the reason why I participated in the detention. I realized that I could call attention to the irony of this situation, the freedom to assemble, in a manner a student could never hope to accomplish. I served the detention because I wanted the young man to know that I supported his decision to skip the program. I wanted to stand in solidarity with him.

I served the detention to challenge others to take a stand, to step out and join their brothers and sisters who suffer because they are not in positions of power and therefore are oppressed. I served the detention because I am convinced that change can come about through nonviolent means.

The Freedom to Assemble

At exactly 3:00 P.M. I reported to the designated location in order to receive my detention duties. The students reporting to serve detention assumed that I was the detention supervisor and refused to accept the explanation of why I was present, until the young man stated, "No, he's here with me." With a degree of reluctance the supervising instructor placed me under the guidance of the custodian. Again, I was reminded of my position of power as the custodian was extremely hesitant to assign any tasks. My first task consisted of collecting and emptying the recycling boxes, which was followed by the task of emptying and re-bagging the garbage cans. Entering the classrooms of fellow staff members provided an opportunity to discuss the events of Tuesday and explain why I needed to serve this detention. Some of the teachers responded with a nervous laugh, others confessed that they too skipped the program, and some dismissed me as a lunatic as they returned to the scholarly work of searching the internet. As we drifted from classroom to classroom pushing the oversized garbage bin, I found myself wondering what the administration hoped to accomplish by having this young man serve detention. Were these sixty minutes of oppression intended to make him appreciate the opportunity, the freedom, to assemble? Were the names and memories of dead soldiers supposed to fill his thoughts? Was picking gum off the bottom of a garbage can supposed to ignite the fire of patriotism in his belly? Or was this to be a simple reminder for this young man that you do not have the freedom to question or challenge the authority of the administration even though you live in America. The administration reported, we have the freedom to assemble,

SO, I am ordering you to assemble in the name of educational opportunities.

At the completion of the hour we reported to the supervisor's classroom, recorded the time and initialed all the proper squares. As the young man and I passed through the doorway the supervisor asked, "Will you attend the Veterans Day program in the future?" In union we sang, "No." As I turned and strolled down the hall to the right and the young man to the left I thought to myself, they can't force me to assemble and they can't stop me from standing in solidarity with another.

Because we do reside in America, because thousands and thousands of young men and women have given their lives, it is time that we practice our freedom and stand with those who are oppressed. It is time that we acknowledge our positions of privilege and use it for the benefit of others. It is time that we open our mouths to name the injustice in our midst. It is time that we dirty our hands in the garbage cans of our communities in order to establish a better, cleaner, community for everyone. It is time that we serve a detention, or two or three, or. . .

> *"We do not think the Constitution recognizes a generalized right of 'social association' that includes chance encounters in dance halls."*

Age Restrictions Do Not Violate First Amendment Associational Rights of Minors

The Supreme Court's Decision

William Rehnquist

In the following viewpoint William Rehnquist, writing for the majority of the US Supreme Court, argues that a Texas law setting an age restriction in dance halls does not violate the First Amendment associational rights of minors. Rehnquist claims that a law setting an age restriction such as this impinges upon neither intimate association nor expressive association: the two senses of association recognized by the Court as constitutionally protected. In light of the lack of constitutional right, Rehnquist claims that the city's justification for the law seems perfectly reasonable. Rehnquist was appointed to the US Supreme Court by President Richard Nixon in 1972 and became chief justice in 1986, serving in this role until his retirement in 2005.

Petitioner city of Dallas adopted an ordinance restricting admission to certain dance halls to persons between the ages of 14 and 18. Respondent, the owner of one of these "teenage" dance halls, sued to contest the constitutional validity of the ordinance. The Texas Court of Appeals held that the ordinance violated the First Amendment right of persons between the ages of 14 and 18 to associate with persons outside that age group. We now reverse, holding that the First Amendment secures no such right.

The Dallas Ordinance

In 1985, in response to requests for dance halls open only to teenagers, the city of Dallas authorized the licensing of "Class E" dance halls. The purpose of the ordinance was to provide a place where teenagers could socialize with each other, but not be subject to the potentially detrimental influences of older teenagers and young adults. The provision of the ordinance at issue here, Dallas City Code 14-8.1 (1985), restricts the ages of admission to Class E dance halls to persons between the ages of 14 and 18. This provision, as enacted, restricted admission to those between 14 and 17, but it was subsequently amended to include 18-year-olds. Parents, guardians, law enforcement, and dance-hall personnel are excepted from the ordinance's age restriction. The ordinance also limits the hours of operation of Class E dance halls to between 1 P.M. and midnight daily when school is not in session.

Respondent operates the Twilight Skating Rink in Dallas and obtained a license for a Class E dance hall. He divided the floor of his roller-skating rink into two sections with moveable plastic cones or pylons. On one side of the pylons, persons between the ages of 14 and 18 dance, while on the other side, persons of all ages skate to the same music—usually soul and "funk" music played by a disc jockey. No age or hour restrictions are applicable to the skating rink. Respondent does not serve alcohol on the premises, and security personnel are present. The Twilight does not have a selective admissions policy. It charges between $3.50

In 1989 the Supreme Court ruled that laws setting an age restriction at Dallas, Texas, dance halls do not violate the First Amendment associational rights of minors. © Brand New Images/ Getty Images.

and $5 per person for admission to the dance hall and between $2.50 and $5 per person for admission to the skating rink. Most of the patrons are strangers to each other, and the establishment serves as many as 1,000 customers per night.

Respondent sued in the District Court of Dallas County to enjoin enforcement of the age and hour restrictions of the ordinance. He contended that the ordinance violated substantive due process and equal protection under the United States and Texas Constitutions, and that it unconstitutionally infringed the rights of persons between the ages of 14 and 17 (now 18) to associate with persons outside that age bracket. The trial court upheld the ordinance, finding that it was rationally related to the city's legitimate interest in ensuring the safety and welfare of children.

The Texas Court of Appeals upheld the ordinance's time restriction, but it struck down the age restriction. The Court of Appeals held that the age restriction violated the First Amendment associational rights of minors. To support a restriction on the fundamental right of "social association," the court said that "the legislative body must show a compelling interest," and the regulation "must be accomplished by the least restrictive means." The court recognized the city's interest in "protect[ing] minors from detrimental, corrupting influences," but held that the "City's stated purposes . . . may be achieved in ways that are less intrusive on minors' freedom to associate." The Court of Appeals stated that "[a] child's right of association may not be abridged simply on the premise that he 'might' associate with those who would persuade him into bad habits," and that "neither the activity of dancing per se, nor association of children aged fourteen through eighteen with persons of other ages in the context of dancing renders such children peculiarly vulnerable to the evils that defendant City seeks to prevent." We granted certiorari [review], and now reverse.

The Right of Association

The dispositive question in this case is the level of judicial "scrutiny" to be applied to the city's ordinance. Unless laws "create suspect classifications or impinge upon constitutionally protected rights" [*San Antonio Independent School Dist. v. Rodriguez* (1973)], it need only be shown that they bear "some rational relationship to a legitimate state purpose." Respondent does not contend that dance-hall patrons are a "suspect classification," but he does urge that the ordinance in question interferes with associational rights of such patrons guaranteed by the First Amendment.

While the First Amendment does not in terms protect a "right of association," our cases have recognized that it embraces such a right in certain circumstances. In *Roberts v. United States Jaycees* (1984), we noted two different sorts of "freedom of association" that are protected by the United States Constitution:

> Our decisions have referred to constitutionally protected 'freedom of association' in two distinct senses. In one line of

decisions, the Court has concluded that choices to enter into and maintain certain intimate human relationships must be secured against undue intrusion by the State because of the role of such relationships in safeguarding the individual freedom that is central to our constitutional scheme. In this respect, freedom of association receives protection as a fundamental element of personal liberty. In another set of decisions, the Court has recognized a right to associate for the purpose of engaging in those activities protected by the First Amendment—speech, assembly, petition for the redress of grievances, and the exercise of religion.

Neither Intimate nor Expressive Association

It is clear beyond cavil that dance-hall patrons, who may number 1,000 on any given night, are not engaged in the sort of "intimate human relationships" referred to in *Roberts*. The Texas Court of Appeals, however, thought that such patrons were engaged in a form of expressive activity that was protected by the First Amendment. We disagree.

The Dallas ordinance restricts attendance at Class E dance halls to minors between the ages of 14 and 18 and certain excepted adults. It thus limits the minors' ability to dance with adults who may not attend, and it limits the opportunity of such adults to dance with minors. These opportunities might be described as "associational" in common parlance, but they simply do not involve the sort of expressive association that the First Amendment has been held to protect. The hundreds of teenagers who congregate each night at this particular dance hall are not members of any organized association; they are patrons of the same business establishment. Most are strangers to one another, and the dance hall admits all who are willing to pay the admission fee. There is no suggestion that these patrons "take positions on public questions" or perform any of the other similar activities described in *Board of Directors of Rotary International v. Rotary Club of Duarte* (1987).

The US Supreme Court on Children and Adults

The state's authority over children's activities is broader than over like actions of adults. This is peculiarly true of public activities and in matters of employment. A democratic society rests, for its continuance, upon the healthy, well rounded growth of young people into full maturity as citizens, with all that implies. It may secure this against impeding restraints and dangers within a broad range of selection. Among evils most appropriate for such action are the crippling effects of child employment, more especially in public places, and the possible harms arising from other activities subject to all the diverse influences of the street. It is too late now to doubt that legislation appropriately designed to reach such evils is within the state's police power, whether against the parent's claim to control of the child or one that religious scruples dictate contrary action.

Wiley Rutledge, Majority opinion, Prince v. Massachusetts, *January 31, 1944.*

The cases cited in *Roberts* recognize that "freedom of speech" means more than simply the right to talk and to write. It is possible to find some kernel of expression in almost every activity a person undertakes—for example, walking down the street or meeting one's friends at a shopping mall—but such a kernel is not sufficient to bring the activity within the protection of the First Amendment. We think the activity of these dance-hall patrons—coming together to engage in recreational dancing—is not protected by the First Amendment. Thus this activity qualifies neither as a form of "intimate association" nor as a form of "expressive association" as those terms were described in *Roberts.*

Unlike the Court of Appeals, we do not think the Constitution recognizes a generalized right of "social association" that includes chance encounters in dance halls. The Court of Appeals relied, mistakenly we think, on a statement from our opinion in *Griswold v. Connecticut* (1965), that "[t]he right to freely associate is not limited to 'political' assemblies, but includes those that 'pertain to the social, legal, and economic benefit' of our citizens." But the quoted language from *Griswold* recognizes nothing more than that the right of expressive association extends to groups organized to engage in speech that does not pertain directly to politics.

A Rational Basis for the Law

The Dallas ordinance, therefore, implicates no suspect class and impinges on no constitutionally protected right. The question remaining is whether the classification engaged in by the city survives "rational-basis" scrutiny under the Equal Protection Clause. The city has chosen to impose a rule that separates 14- to 18-year-olds from what may be the corrupting influences of older teenagers and young adults. Ray Couch, an urban planner for the city's Department of Planning and Development, testified:

> [O]lder kids [whom the ordinance prohibits from entering Class E dance halls] can access drugs and alcohol, and they have more mature sexual attitudes, more liberal sexual attitudes in general. . . . And we're concerned about mixing up these [older] individuals with youngsters that [sic] have not fully matured.

A Dallas police officer, Wesley Michael, testified that the age restriction was intended to discourage juvenile crime. Respondent claims that this restriction "has no real connection with the City's stated interests and objectives." Except for saloons and teenage dance halls, respondent argues, teenagers and adults in Dallas may associate with each other, including at the skating area of the Twilight Skating Rink. Respondent also states, as did the court below, that the city can achieve its objectives through increased supervision, education, and prosecution of those who corrupt minors. . . .

As we said in *New Orleans v. Dukes* (1976): "[I]n the local economic sphere, it is only the invidious discrimination, the wholly arbitrary act, which cannot stand consistently with the Fourteenth Amendment." The city could reasonably conclude, as Couch stated, that teenagers might be susceptible to corrupting influences if permitted, unaccompanied by their parents, to frequent a dance hall with older persons. The city could properly conclude that limiting dance-hall contacts between juveniles and adults would make less likely illicit or undesirable juvenile involvement with alcohol, illegal drugs, and promiscuous sex. It is true that the city allows teenagers and adults to roller-skate together, but skating involves less physical contact than dancing. The differences between the two activities may not be striking, but differentiation need not be striking in order to survive rational-basis scrutiny.

We hold that the Dallas ordinance does not infringe on any constitutionally protected right of association, and that a rational relationship exists between the age restriction for Class E dance halls and the city's interest in promoting the welfare of teenagers.

> "We find that the state has demonstrated
> that the curfew ordinance furthers a
> compelling state interest."

Juvenile Curfew Laws Are Constitutional When Employed to Reduce Crime

The Circuit Court's Decision

E. Grady Jolly

In the following viewpoint Judge E. Grady Jolly, writing the majority opinion for the US Court of the Appeals for the Fifth Circuit, contends that a Dallas law establishing a juvenile curfew does not violate the constitutional rights of juveniles. Jolly, assuming that the right to move freely is a fundamental right, scrutinizes the Dallas law to ensure that it promotes a compelling government interest. He concludes that the law does further the city's interest in reducing juvenile crime and promoting the safety of juveniles, while still allowing enough exceptions to accommodate the legitimate late-night activities of juveniles. Jolly is a judge for the United States Court of Appeals for the Fifth Circuit in Jackson, Mississippi.

E. Grady Jolly, Majority opinion, *Qutb v. Strauss*, US Court of the Appeals for the Fifth Circuit, v. 11, November 19, 1993. www.ca5.uscourts.gov. Copyright © 1993 by US Court of Appeals for the Fifth Circuit.

This appeal presents a challenge to the constitutionality of a nocturnal juvenile curfew ordinance enacted by Dallas, Texas. The ordinance makes it a misdemeanor for persons under the age of seventeen to use the city streets or to be present at other public places within the city between certain hours. Several plaintiffs brought suit against the city to strike down the ordinance. The district court ruled for the plaintiffs, holding that the ordinance violated both the United States and the Texas Constitutions, and permanently enjoined enforcement of the ordinance. The city appeals. Because we conclude that this ordinance does not violate the United States or Texas Constitutions, we reverse the district court.

Dallas' Juvenile Curfew Law

On June 12, 1991, in response to citizens' demands for protection of the city's youth, the Dallas City Council enacted a juvenile curfew ordinance. This ordinance prohibits persons under seventeen years of age from remaining in a public place or establishment from 11 P.M. until 6 A.M. on weeknights and from 12 midnight until 6 A.M. on weekends. As defined by the ordinance, a "public place" is any place to which the public or a substantial group of the public has access, and includes streets, highways, and the common areas of schools, hospitals, apartment houses, office buildings, transport facilities, and shops. "Establishment" is defined as "any privately-owned place of business operated for a profit to which the public is invited, including but not limited to any place of amusement or entertainment."

Although the ordinance restricts the hours when minors are allowed in public areas, the ordinance also contains a number of exceptions, or defenses. A person under the age of seventeen in a public place during curfew hours does not violate the ordinance if he or she is accompanied by a parent or guardian, or is on an errand for a parent or guardian. Likewise, minors would be allowed in public places if they are in a motor vehicle travelling to or from a place of employment, or if they are involved in employment related activities. Affected minors could attend school, religious, or civic organizational functions—or generally exercise their First Amendment speech and associational rights—without violating the ordinance. Nor is it a violation to engage in interstate travel, or remain on a sidewalk in front of the minor's home, or the home of a neighbor. And finally, the ordinance places no restrictions on a minor's ability to move about during curfew hours in the case of an emergency.

A minor violates the curfew if he or she remains in any public place or on the premises of any establishment during curfew hours, and if the minors' activities are not exempted from coverage. If a minor is apparently violating the ordinance, the ordinance requires police officers to ask the age of the apparent offender, and to inquire into the reasons for being in a public place during curfew hours before taking any enforcement action. An officer may issue a citation or arrest the apparent offender only if the officer reasonably believes that the person has violated the ordinance and that no defenses apply. If convicted, an offending party is subject to a fine not to exceed $500.00 for each separate offense.

Like minors who have violated the offense, a parent of a minor, or an owner, operator, or employee of a business establishment is also subject to a fine not to exceed $500 for each separate offense. A parent or guardian of a minor violates the ordinance if he or she knowingly permits, or by insufficient control allows, a minor child to remain in any public place or on the premises of any establishment during curfew hours. An owner, operator, or employee of a business establishment commits an offense by knowingly allowing a minor to remain upon the premises of the establishment during curfew hours.

The Plaintiffs' Objection to the Law

On July 3, 1991, two weeks after the ordinance was enacted, Elizabeth Qutb and three other parents filed suit—both individually and as next friends of their teenage children—seeking a

Some courts have ruled that juvenile curfew laws aimed at stopping the nighttime gathering of teenagers are constitutional. © Marvin Joseph/The Washington Post/Getty Images.

temporary restraining order and a permanent injunction against the enforcement of the juvenile curfew ordinance on the basis that the ordinance [was] unconstitutional. . . .

On August 10, 1992, the district court held that the curfew impermissibly restricted minors' First Amendment right to associate, and that it created classifications that could not withstand constitutional scrutiny. Accordingly, the district court permanently enjoined enforcement of the curfew, and the city now appeals.

We review *de novo* [anew] the district court's conclusions of constitutional law. The minor plaintiffs argue, *inter alia* [among other things], that the curfew ordinance violates the Equal Protection Clause of the Fourteenth Amendment. The Equal Protection Clause "is essentially a direction that all persons similarly situated should be treated alike" [*City of Cleburne v. Cleburne Living Ctr., Inc.* (1985)]. Only if the challenged government action classifies or distinguishes between two or more relevant groups must we conduct an equal protection inquiry.

Here, it is clear that the curfew ordinance distinguishes between classes of individuals on the basis of age, treating those persons under the age of seventeen differently from those persons age seventeen and older. Because the curfew ordinance distinguishes between two groups, we must analyze the curfew ordinance under the Equal Protection Clause.

The Proper Standard of Review

Under the Equal Protection analysis, we apply different standards of review depending upon the right or classification involved. If a classification disadvantages a "suspect class" or impinges upon a "fundamental right," the ordinance is subject to strict scrutiny. Under the strict scrutiny standard, we accord the classification no presumption of constitutionality. Instead, we ask whether the classification promotes a compelling governmental interest and, if so, whether the ordinance is narrowly tailored such that there are no less restrictive means available to effectuate the desired end.

In this case, no one has argued, and correctly so, that a classification based on age is a suspect classification. The minor plaintiffs, however, have argued that the curfew ordinance impinges upon their "fundamental right" to move about freely in public. For purposes of our analysis, we assume without deciding that the right to move about freely is a fundamental right. We are mindful, however, that this ordinance is directed solely at the activities of juveniles and, under certain circumstances, minors may be treated differently from adults.

Because we assume that the curfew impinges upon a fundamental right, we will now subject the ordinance to strict scrutiny review. As stated earlier, to survive strict scrutiny, a classification created by the ordinance must promote a compelling governmental interest, and it must be narrowly tailored to achieve this interest. The city's stated interest in enacting the ordinance is to reduce juvenile crime and victimization, while promoting juvenile safety and well-being. The Supreme Court has recognized that the state "has a strong and legitimate interest in the welfare of its young citizens, whose immaturity, inexperience, and lack of judgment may sometimes impair their ability to exercise their rights wisely" [*Hodgson v. Minnesota* (1990)]. In this case, the plaintiffs concede and the district court [holds] that the state's interest in this case is compelling. Given the fact that the state's interest is elevated by the minority status of the affected persons, we have no difficulty agreeing with the parties and with the district court.

The City's Justification for the Curfew

In the light of the state's compelling interest in increasing juvenile safety and decreasing juvenile crime, we must now determine whether the curfew ordinance is narrowly tailored to achieve that interest. The district court held that the city "totally failed to establish that the ordinance's classification between minors and non-minors is narrowly tailored to achieve the stated goals of the curfew." We disagree.

To be narrowly tailored, there must be a nexus between the stated government interest and the classification created by the ordinance. This test "ensures that the means chosen 'fit' this compelling goal so closely that there is little or no possibility that the motive for the classification was illegitimate. . . ." [*City of Richmond v. J.A. Croson, Co.* (1989)].

The articulated purpose of the curfew ordinance enacted by the city of Dallas is to protect juveniles from harm, and to reduce juvenile crime and violence occurring in the city. The ordinance's distinction based upon age furthers these objectives. Before the district court, the city presented the following statistical information:

1. Juvenile crime increases proportionally with age between ten years old and sixteen years old.

2. In 1989, Dallas recorded 5,160 juvenile arrests, while in 1990 there were 5,425 juvenile arrests. In 1990 there were forty murders, ninety-one sex offenses, 233 robberies, and 230 aggravated assaults committed by juveniles.

From January 1991 through April 1991, juveniles were arrested for twenty-one murders, thirty sex offenses, 128 robberies, 107 aggravated assaults, and 1,042 crimes against property.

3. Murders are most likely to occur between 10:00 P.M. and 1:00 A.M. and most likely to occur in apartments and apartment parking lots and streets and highways.

4. Aggravated assaults are most likely to occur between 11:00 P.M. and 1:00 A.M.

5. Rapes are most likely to occur between 1:00 A.M. and 3:00 A.M. and sixteen percent of rapes occur on public streets and highways.

6. Thirty-one percent of robberies occur on streets and highways.

Although the city was unable to provide precise data concerning the number of juveniles who commit crimes during the curfew hours, or the number of juvenile victims of crimes committed during the curfew, the city nonetheless provided sufficient data to demonstrate that the classification created by the ordinance "fits" the state's compelling interest. . . .

Exceptions to the Curfew Law

With the ordinance before us today, the city of Dallas has created a nocturnal juvenile curfew that satisfies strict scrutiny. By including the defenses to a violation of the ordinance, the city has enacted a narrowly drawn ordinance that allows the city to meet its stated goals while respecting the rights of the affected minors. As the city points out, a juvenile may move about freely in Dallas if accompanied by a parent or a guardian, or a person at least eighteen years of age who is authorized by a parent or guardian to have custody of the minor. If the juvenile is traveling interstate, returning from a school-sponsored function, a civic organization-sponsored function, or a religious function, or going home after work, the ordinance does not apply. If the juvenile is

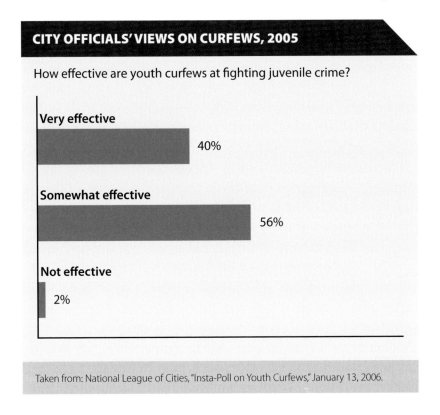

CITY OFFICIALS' VIEWS ON CURFEWS, 2005

How effective are youth curfews at fighting juvenile crime?

Very effective

40%

Somewhat effective

56%

Not effective

2%

Taken from: National League of Cities, "Insta-Poll on Youth Curfews," January 13, 2006.

on an errand for his or her parent or guardian, the ordinance does not apply. If the juvenile is involved in an emergency, the ordinance does not apply. If the juvenile is on a sidewalk in front of his or her home *or* the home of a neighbor, the ordinance does not apply. Most notably, if the juvenile is exercising his or her First Amendment rights, the curfew ordinance does not apply.

Against the ordinance's expansive list of defenses, the district court attempted to provide examples of activities with which the curfew ordinance would interfere. The district court suggested the example of "a midnight basketball league aimed solely at keeping juveniles off of the streets" to demonstrate that participation in legitimate desirable activities would violate the ordinance unless the activities were officially organized, sponsored, or supervised by the city, a school, a civic association, or some "other entity." In its effort to demonstrate that the ordinance was overly broad, the district court referred to concerts, movies, plays, study groups, or church activities that may extend past curfew hours. The district court finally noted that "every juvenile in the city could be arrested and fined up to $500.00 upon conviction if he or she merely sought to take an innocent stroll or 'gaze at the stars from a public park.'"

With due respect to the able district court, we are convinced that upon examination its analysis collapses. It is true, of course, that the curfew ordinance would restrict some late-night activities of juveniles; if indeed it did not, then there would be no purpose in enacting it. But when balanced with the compelling interest sought to be addressed—protecting juveniles and preventing juvenile crime—the impositions are minor. The district court failed to observe that none of the activities it listed are restricted if the juvenile is accompanied by a parent or a guardian. Even if the child is unaccompanied by a parent or a guardian, we can presume that most events such as a "midnight basketball league" or a church youth group outing ordinarily would be organized, sponsored or supervised by an adult or an organization, and these are exceptions to the curfew. Although it is true that in some situations unaccompanied juveniles may be forced to attend early evening features of a movie or leave a play or concert before its conclusion, this imposition is ameliorated by several of the ordinance's defenses so that the juvenile is not deprived of actually attending such cultural and entertainment opportunities. Furthermore, a juvenile can take an "innocent stroll" and stare at the stars until 11:00 on week-nights and until 12:00 midnight on weekends; indeed, a juvenile may stare at the stars all night long from the front sidewalk of his or her home or the home of a neighbor. Thus, after carefully examining the juvenile curfew ordinance enacted by the city of Dallas, we conclude that it is narrowly tailored to address the city's compelling interest and any burden this ordinance places upon minors' constitutional rights will be minimal. . . .

In conclusion, we find that the state has demonstrated that the curfew ordinance furthers a compelling state interest, i.e., protecting juveniles from crime on the streets. We further conclude that the ordinance is narrowly tailored to achieve this compelling state interest. Accordingly, we hold that the nocturnal juvenile curfew ordinance enacted by the city of Dallas is constitutional.

"The City's failure to provide adequate exceptions not only excessively burdens minors' right to free movement, but it also excessively burdens their right to free speech."

Juvenile Curfew Laws Without Adequate Exceptions Are Unconstitutional

The Circuit Court's Decision

Charles Wiggins

In the following viewpoint Charles Wiggins, writing for the US Court of Appeals for the Ninth Circuit, finds a juvenile curfew law in San Diego, California, to be unconstitutional. Wiggins argues that the government may constrain minors' rights, but only if it has a compelling interest and does not impose limits that are broader than necessary. Whereas Wiggins finds the goal of reducing crime legitimate, he finds San Diego's curfew law lacking in adequate exceptions for activities protected by the US Constitution. Wiggins served as a judge for the US Court of Appeals for the Ninth Circuit from the time of his appointment in 1984 by President Ronald Reagan until his death in 2000.

The City of San Diego enacted its juvenile curfew ordinance in 1947. The ordinance reads as follows:

> It shall be unlawful for any minor under the age of eighteen (18) years, to loiter, idle, wander, stroll or play in or upon the public streets, highways, roads, alleys, parks, playgrounds, wharves, docks, or other public grounds, public places and public buildings, places of amusement and entertainment, vacant lots or other unsupervised places, between the hours of ten o'clock P.M. and daylight immediately following.

The ordinance then provides that the curfew does not apply in four situations:

> (1) "when the minor is accompanied by his or her parents, guardian, or other adult person having the care and custody of the minor,"
>
> (2) "when the minor is upon an emergency errand directed by his or her parent or guardian or other adult person having the care and custody of the minor,"
>
> (3) "when the minor is returning directly home from a meeting, entertainment or recreational activity directed, supervised or sponsored by the local educational authorities," or
>
> (4) "when the presence of such minor in said place or places is connected with and required by some legitimate business, trade, profession or occupation in which said minor is lawfully engaged."

A minor violating § 58.01 commits a misdemeanor. Section 58.01.1 also creates criminal liability for the "parent, guardian or other adult person having the care and custody of a minor" who permits or allows the minor to violate the curfew ordinance. On April 25, 1994, the City adopted a resolution to enforce the curfew aggressively.

The Rights of Minors

Plaintiffs are minors and parents of minors from San Diego. They brought an action under 42 U.S.C. § 1983 to challenge the ordinance's constitutionality on its face. Plaintiff minors allege, among other things, that the ordinance restricts them from many otherwise lawful activities after curfew hours, i.e., volunteering at a homeless shelter, attending concerts as a music critic, studying with other students, meeting with friends at their homes or in coffee houses, stopping at a restaurant to eat dinner after serving on the School District Board, auditioning for theater parts, attending ice hockey practice, practicing astronomy, and dancing at an under-21 dance club. . . .

Although many federal courts have recognized that juvenile curfews implicate the fundamental rights of minors, the parties dispute whether strict scrutiny review is necessary. The Supreme Court teaches that rights are no less "fundamental" for minors than adults, but that the analysis of those rights may differ:

> Constitutional rights do not mature and come into being magically only when one attains the state-defined age of majority. Minors, as well as adults, are protected by the Constitution and possess constitutional rights. The Court indeed, however, long has recognized that the State has somewhat broader authority to regulate the activities of children than of adults. It remains, then, to examine whether there is any significant state interest in [the effect of the statute] that is not present in the case of an adult [*Planned Parenthood of Cent. Missouri v. Danforth* (1976) (citations omitted)]. Thus, minors' rights are not coextensive with the rights of adults because the state has a greater range of interests that justify the infringement of minors' rights.

The Supreme Court has articulated [in *Bellotti v. Baird* (1979)] three specific factors that, when applicable, warrant differential analysis of the constitutional rights of minors and adults: (1) the peculiar vulnerability of children; (2) their inability to make critical decisions in an informed, mature manner; and (3) the importance of the parental role in child rearing. The *Bellotti* test does not establish a lower level of scrutiny for the constitutional rights of minors in the context of a juvenile curfew. Rather, the *Bellotti* framework enables courts to determine whether the state has a compelling interest justifying greater restrictions on minors than on adults. . . .

A Compelling Governmental Interest

The ostensible purposes of the ordinance identified by the City in its brief are to protect children from nighttime dangers, to reduce juvenile crime, and to involve parents in control of their children. At oral argument, the City admitted that its "compelling interest is, quite frankly, to reduce gang activity." As the City also admits, however, the ordinance is not limited to gang activities.

The City has a compelling interest in protecting the entire community from crime, including juvenile crime. The City's interest in protecting the safety and welfare of its minors is also a compelling interest. The fact that much of the perceived danger stems from gang activity does not lessen the nature of the City's interest in protecting the safety and welfare of minors, although it may affect the analysis of whether the ordinance is narrowly tailored. . .

The City has established some nexus between the curfew and its compelling interest of reducing juvenile crime and victimization. This is particularly true because of our conclusion that minors have a special vulnerability to the dangers of the streets at night. We will not dismiss the City's legislative conclusion that the curfew will have a salutary effect on juvenile crime and victimization.

The Scope of the Exceptions

In order to be narrowly tailored, the ordinance must ensure that the broad curfew minimizes any burden on minors' fundamental rights, such as the right to free movement. Thus, we examine the ordinance's exceptions to determine whether they sufficiently exempt legitimate activities from the curfew. . . .

Clearly, San Diego could have enacted a narrower curfew ordinance that would pass constitutional muster. Its present ordinance is problematic because it does not provide exceptions for many legitimate activities, with or without parental permission. This is true even though minors may be uniquely vulnerable at night; the curfew's blanket coverage restricts participation in, and travel to or from, many legitimate recreational activities even those that may not expose their special vulnerability. In this regard, it is significant that San Diego rejected a proposal to tailor the ordinance more narrowly by adopting the broader exceptions used in the ordinance upheld in *Qutb* [*v. Strauss* (5th cir. 1993)]. The City's failure to provide adequate exceptions not only excessively burdens minors' right to free movement, but it also

The City of San Diego enacted its juvenile curfew ordinance in 1947, and in 1997 the US Court of Appeals for the Ninth Circuit found it to be unconstitutional. © John Eder/Getty Images.

excessively burdens their right to free speech, as explained in our separate discussion of the First Amendment. . . .

We therefore conclude that the City has not shown that the curfew is a close fit to the problem of juvenile crime and victimization because the curfew sweeps broadly, with few exceptions for otherwise legitimate activity. The broad sweep of the ordinance is particularly marked for an ordinance aimed, as the City admitted, at illegal gang activity. The district court in *Waters* [*v. Barry* (D.D.C. 1989)] eloquently explained the constitutional difficulty with a juvenile curfew lacking adequate exceptions:

> The Court recognizes that, in the eyes of many, the crippling effects of crime demand stern responses. With the Act, however, the District has chosen to address the problem through means that are stern to the point of unconstitutionality. Rather than a narrowly drawn, constitutionally sensitive response, the District has effectively chosen to deal with the problem by making thousands of this city's innocent juveniles prisoners at night in their homes.

We conclude that the ordinance is not narrowly tailored to meet the City's compelling interests, as required by strict scrutiny. Thus, we hold that the ordinance is unconstitutional even if given a broad construction to avoid vagueness problems.

The First Amendment Rights of Minors

We now explain our conclusion regarding plaintiff minors' fundamental First Amendment rights, which are incorporated against the states by the Fourteenth Amendment. Specifically, we address whether the ordinance's restrictions on legitimate exercise of minors' First Amendment rights makes the ordinance unconstitutionally overbroad. . . .

Minors, like adults, have a fundamental right to freedom of expression. Expression includes speech and expressive conduct. Thus, a facial First Amendment challenge to an ordinance can be brought against regulation of "spoken words" or where a statute

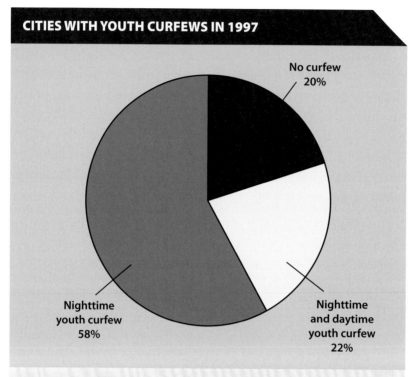

CITIES WITH YOUTH CURFEWS IN 1997

No curfew
20%

Nighttime
youth curfew
58%

Nighttime
and daytime
youth curfew
22%

Taken from: US Conference of Mayors, *A Status Report on Youth Curfews in America's Cities: A 347-City Survey*, 1997.

by its terms regulates the time, place and manner of expressive or communicative conduct. . . .

Having concluded a First Amendment facial challenge is permissible, we apply the traditional three-part test to determine whether the ordinance is a reasonable time, place, and manner restriction: (1) it must be content neutral; (2) it must be narrowly tailored to a significant government interest; and (3) it must leave open ample alternative channels for legitimate expression. It is undisputed that the regulation is content neutral. Plaintiffs contend that ordinance fails the other two prongs of the test.

For First Amendment purposes, the physical and psychological well-being of minors is a compelling government interest. Thus, the ordinance must be narrowly tailored to achieve that interest. We hold the ordinance is not narrowly tailored because it does not sufficiently exempt legitimate First Amendment activities from the curfew. The City argues in its brief that "a broad First Amendment expression exception would effectively reduce a curfew ordinance to a useless device." This admission destroys an argument that the City narrowly tailored its ordinance to serve its compelling interest in minors' well-being while imposing only a minimal burden on their First Amendment rights. The City did not create a robust, or even minimal, First Amendment exception to permit minors to express themselves during curfew hours without the supervision of a parent or guardian, apparently preferring instead to have no First Amendment exception at all. This is not narrow tailoring. We therefore need not reach the question of whether the ordinance leaves open adequate alternative channels of expression. The ordinance is not a reasonable time, place, and manner restriction under the First Amendment.

The parties also dispute whether the First Amendment is implicated by the ordinance's restrictions on minors' right of association. The Supreme Court has identified two types of recognized rights of association: (1) intimacy; and (2) "expressive association" for First Amendment activity. The right to expressive association includes assemblies for non-political purposes, such as social, legal, or economic ones, although the Constitution does not provide a generalized right to societal association outside the context of expressive association ... The curfew does not provide any exemption even for "expressive association." ...

We hold that the ordinance is unconstitutional. When construed in a way that avoids unconstitutional vagueness, it is not narrowly tailored to minimize the burden on minors' fundamental constitutional rights.

| "Such a serious circuit split on such widespread legislation deserves attention by the Supreme Court."

The Courts Are Split on the Constitutionality of Juvenile Curfew Laws

Harvard Law Review

In the following viewpoint a member of the Harvard Law Review *argues that the federal circuit courts' treatment of juvenile curfew legislation has been inconsistent and widely divergent. The author claims that the courts provide varied treatment of children's rights, with some courts reviewing juvenile curfew laws more stringently than others because of the rights such laws limit. Surveying several recent circuit cases on the issue of youth curfews, the author concludes that the US Supreme Court should hear a case on juvenile curfews and give conclusive guidance on the treatment of minors' rights in this context.* Harvard Law Review *is a monthly legal journal run by students at Harvard University Law School.*

In 1976, the Supreme Court denied *certiorari* [review] in *Bykofsky v. Borough of Middletown*, the federal courts' first case involving juvenile curfews. In the nearly three decades since, the federal circuits have fragmented over the constitutionality of such laws. Justified on the basis that keeping children off the streets prevents them from engaging in crime or being victimized, juvenile curfews forbid minors to be in public at night except under special circumstances. Some argue that this restriction not only denies minors the basic freedom to be out at night with parental consent, but also impinges on more fundamental aspects of liberty, such as political activism and community involvement. Given that juvenile curfews have become pervasive in recent years and that they enjoy extraordinary popularity, the stakeholders in the question of curfews' constitutionality are numerous indeed.

The Popularity of Juvenile Curfews

Faced with the overwhelming political popularity of juvenile curfews, advocates of minors' rights have attacked the ordinances in court, alleging that the freedoms they restrict are constitutionally protected rights. The federal circuits are inconsistent on the proper treatment of these claims: not only do they disagree on exactly what freedoms are at issue and how fundamental they are, but they also have applied varying levels of scrutiny—with different results—when determining whether those freedoms are unconstitutionally burdened. Because even those circuits hostile to non-emergency juvenile curfews have not rejected them as inherently unconstitutional, the question presented by this fractured doctrine is not whether juvenile curfews are constitutional, but rather, what juvenile curfews are constitutional. The Fifth Circuit's 1993 ruling in *Qutb v. Strauss*, which held that Dallas's juvenile curfew ordinance survived strict scrutiny, provided a model ordinance for other communities. Recently, however, that model has been threatened, particularly by the Second Circuit's decision in *Ramos v. Town of Vernon*, which imposed high statistical requirements for justifying curfews. Because the Supreme Court has never harmonized the circuits' discordant voices, it is difficult to hear any clear legal message. . . .

In the 1990s, not long after federal courts began to develop case law on juvenile curfews, juvenile victimization and crime rates seemed to explode across the country. It is therefore not surprising that juvenile curfews were widely sought, with support crossing political and racial lines. Advocates viewed them as a necessary step toward saving America's imperiled youth and stopping epidemic juvenile crime, though detractors [Craig Hemmens and Katherine Bennett] charged that curfews were little more than "a cosmetic 'quick-fix' response to what is perceived to be a serious problem." By 1995, 77% of cities with populations greater than 200,000 had some form of juvenile curfew, 60% of which were either enacted or enhanced after 1990. The popularity of curfews was not limited to large cities: in 1995, 73% of cities of more than 100,000 had curfews, and by 1997, 80% of communities with populations greater than 30,000 had curfews. Over the course of a century, America effectively closed the nighttime streets to minors.

Many current juvenile curfews are modeled after the Dallas curfew that survived strict scrutiny in *Qutb*. Such curfews forbid unaccompanied minors—those younger than seventeen or eighteen—from being in public spaces late at night, usually between 11 P.M. and 6 A.M. during the week, and midnight and 6 A.M. on weekends. The curfews typically have exceptions for minors who are on the street due to emergency, work reasons, interstate travel, attendance of a sponsored event, participation in First Amendment activities, or an errand for a parent. The stated rationales for juvenile curfews usually include reducing crime (particularly by disrupting the formation of gangs), protecting children, and increasing parental responsibility. . . .

The Rights of Children

At the heart of juvenile curfew challenges is the assertion that minors have a constitutional right to be on the streets at night.

ENACTMENT OF JUVENILE CURFEW LAWS

According to a 2005 poll of mayors and city officials of cities that have curfews:

67% enacted their juvenile curfews in the past 20 years

38% enacted their juvenile curfews in the past 10 years

Taken from: National League of Cities, "Youth Curfews Continue to Show Promise," January 13, 2006 (Insta-Poll on Youth Curfews).

The Supreme Court has made clear that children have some sort of rights. In *In re Gault* [1967], the Court held that "whatever may be their precise impact, neither the Fourteenth Amendment nor the Bill of Rights is for adults alone." Likewise, in *Planned Parenthood of Central Missouri v. Danforth* [1976], the Court reasoned that "[c]onstitutional rights do not mature and come into being magically only when one attains the state-defined age of majority." On the other hand, the Court has indicated that the rights of minors are not equivalent to those of adults. In *Prince v. Massachusetts* [1944], for example, it held that "[t]he state's authority over children's activities is broader than over the like actions of adults," and in *Ginsberg v. New York* [1968], the Court upheld a state law that limited minors' access to pornography, even while acknowledging that such a law would have been unconstitutional if applied to adults.

The Supreme Court consistently has denied *certiorari* [review] in juvenile curfew cases, leaving the federal circuits to fend for themselves in determining the appropriate level of scrutiny for adjudicating these claims. The circuits, predictably, have come to divergent conclusions. The Ninth Circuit found strict scrutiny appropriate. The Fourth Circuit identified intermediate or heightened scrutiny as the appropriate level. The Second Circuit adopted what seems to be a modified version of intermediate scrutiny. Finally, a plurality of the D.C. Circuit reasoned that rational basis review was appropriate.

The confusion in the circuits stems from their different approaches to minors' rights. Because age is not a suspect classification, equal protection challenges to juvenile curfews must allege that the ordinances burden a fundamental right—the right of free movement. To determine whether and to what extent minors have such a right, the circuits have looked to Supreme Court precedents, particularly to *Bellotti v. Baird*.

The *Bellotti* Framework

In 1979, the plurality opinion in *Bellotti* established a new guide for charting the uncertain territory of minors' rights. The *Bellotti* Court examined a statute that limited minors' access to abortions and concluded that it was unconstitutional because it required parental consent and provided no judicial bypass for those cases in which a court determined the minor to be mature and fully competent. More significant to this Note than *Bellotti*'s holding was the plurality's discussion of children's constitutional rights. The plurality offered "three reasons justifying [its] conclusion that the constitutional rights of children cannot be equated with those of adults: the peculiar vulnerability of children; their inability to make critical decisions in an informed, mature manner; and the importance of the parental role in child rearing." With regard to the second factor, the plurality emphasized that "minors often lack the experience, perspective, and judgment to . . . avoid choices that could be detrimental to them."

Because the *Bellotti* plurality drew its three factors out of diverse cases involving the rights of minors and not merely out of cases pertaining to abortion rights, the opinion potentially provides a framework for assessing all minors' rights claims. Thus, although some commentators and courts have argued that *Bellotti's* logic is "troublesome outside of the particular setting of abortion rights" [*Village of Deerfield v. Greenberg* (III. App.Ct. 1990)] most federal courts have found the framework useful when considering the constitutionality of juvenile curfews. The actual application of the *Bellotti* factors in challenges to juvenile curfews, however, has proven both contentious and inconsistent. . . .

Cases in the Federal Courts

The early history of juvenile curfews in the federal courts is reflected in three cases. In *Bykofsky v. Borough of Middletown*, the Middle District of Pennsylvania held that because minors had a diminished interest in being out at night, "legislation peculiarly applicable to minors is warranted for the protection of the public—e.g., to protect the community from youths aimlessly roaming the streets during the nighttime hours." In *Johnson v. Opelousas* [1981], however, the Fifth Circuit struck down as overbroad a curfew similar to the one upheld in *Bykofsky* because the curfew provided no exception for minors attending religious or school meetings, sitting on their own sidewalks, going to or from their jobs, or engaging in interstate travel. Twelve years later, in *Qutb v. Strauss*, the Fifth Circuit upheld a Dallas curfew designed precisely to address the concerns raised in *Johnson*. The *Qutb* court ruled that the curfew ordinance would survive even under strict scrutiny, and accordingly declined to decide the appropriate level of review. Because of *Qutb's* strong holding, Dallas's curfew became the model used by most cities and the paradigm against which alternative ordinances were judged. The cases since *Qutb* have plotted an uncertain course.

1. *Nunez v. City of San Diego* [1997]. In *Nunez*, the Ninth Circuit struck down San Diego's juvenile curfew on both equal protection and First Amendment grounds. The court applied strict scrutiny, reasoning that the curfew implicated fundamental

rights and that *Bellotti* should be used to strengthen the state's interest, not to decrease the level of scrutiny. Although San Diego had "established some nexus between the curfew and its compelling interest of reducing juvenile crime and victimization," the City's failure to adopt the *Qutb* exceptions, particularly the First Amendment exception, showed that the curfew was not as narrowly tailored as it could have been. Accordingly, the curfew failed constitutional analysis.

2. *Schleifer v. City of Charlottesville* [1998]. In *Schleifer*, the Fourth Circuit held that Charlottesville's juvenile curfew survived intermediate scrutiny. The court reasoned that this standard was appropriate because although minors have certain liberty interests, these rights are less fundamental than those of adults. Remarking that the "dispute about the desirability or ultimate efficacy of a curfew is a political debate, not a judicial one," the court noted that cities have the right to "not have their efforts at reducing juvenile violence shut down by a court before they even have a chance to make a difference." Ultimately, the court upheld the ordinance, which was modeled after Dallas's curfew, demanding only that the "curfew . . . be shown to be a meaningful step towards solving a real, not fanciful problem."

3. *Hutchins v. District of Columbia* [1999]. In *Hutchins*, the D.C. Circuit, sitting *en banc* [all judges] upheld the District's juvenile curfew, which was almost identical to Dallas's curfew. A plurality of the circuit found rational basis review appropriate because "juveniles do not have a fundamental right to be on the streets at night without adult supervision." Applying the first approach to *Bellotti*, a majority of the court agreed that no more than intermediate scrutiny was required: "[*Bellotti*] means, at a minimum, that a lesser degree of scrutiny is appropriate when evaluating restrictions on minors' activities where their unique vulnerability, immaturity, and need for parental guidance warrant increased state oversight." The court held that the District had demonstrated that its "important government interest" in "protecting the welfare of minors" was sufficient to withstand

Teenagers protest a curfew on the Sunset Strip in Los Angeles. The federal circuit courts' treatment of juvenile curfew legislation has been inconsistent and widely divergent. © AP Photo.

such scrutiny in light of the "reams of evidence depicting the devastating impact of juvenile crime and victimization in the District."

4. *Ramos v. Town of Vernon.* In *Ramos*, the Second Circuit likewise applied intermediate scrutiny, rejecting rational basis review because intermediate scrutiny "allows for a more discerning inquiry to accommodate competing interests," and rejecting strict scrutiny because "[y]outh-blindness is not a constitutional goal." Under the *Ramos* court's conception of intermediate scrutiny, a curfew is more likely to pass constitutional muster "[i]f the direct and primary beneficiaries are children," which Vernon failed to prove. The court emphasized that communities must rely on reasoned analysis and "careful study of the problem" rather than on "stereotypes and assumptions about young people." Vernon had not done so, and its curfew therefore failed intermediate scrutiny.

5. *Hodgkins v. Peterson* [2004]. In *Hodgkins*, the Seventh Circuit held that Indianapolis's juvenile curfew violated minors' First Amendment rights. Although the curfew pursued significant governmental purposes and had a First Amendment exception, the court held that the ordinance was not narrowly

tailored and failed to allow alternative channels for expression. The court feared that minors would be stopped and possibly arrested before they were able to prove that their activities fell within the First Amendment exception, and that this risk would chill nighttime expressive activity. A curfew that "specifie[d] that a law enforcement official must look into whether an affirmative defense applies before making an arrest" could pass muster, but Indianapolis's did not.

The Need for Clarity

The outcomes of these cases indicate that, despite significant disagreement among the circuits regarding the appropriate level of scrutiny, the Dallas model remains effective, having survived challenges in *Schleifer* and *Hutchins*. Likewise, the curfew in *Nunez* failed at least in part because "San Diego rejected a proposal to tailor the ordinance more narrowly by adopting the broader exceptions used in the ordinance upheld in *Qutb*." Although a model ordinance failed scrutiny in *Hodgkins*, this case represents an outlier in its First Amendment concerns. Thus, of greatest significance is *Ramos*, in which a curfew modeled after *Qutb* failed. The *Ramos* court purported to base its equal protection decision on the weakness of the Town's evidence in support of its curfew, particularly on the Town's failure to present statistical evidence about local youth victimization and juvenile delinquency. For *Ramos* to make sense within the larger framework of precedent regarding juvenile curfews, then, the evidence offered by Vernon must have differed in a meaningful way from that offered by Dallas, Charlottesville, and San Diego. . . . However, the evidence offered by those cities was not meaningfully different from that offered by Vernon and hence logically would not have satisfied the *Ramos* court. . . .

Although it is possible to create some coherence in the doctrine by focusing on the Dallas ordinance at issue in *Qutb*, the circuits remain undeniably split on the constitutionality of juvenile curfews. The split involves wildly varying standards of review, significant disagreement over the rights at issue, and dramatic differences in the way in which cities must prove the need for a curfew. Such a serious circuit split on such widespread legislation deserves attention by the Supreme Court. The Court should take up the challenge raised by Justice [Thurgood] Marshall in response to *Bykofsky v. Borough of Middletown* and determine the answer to this "substantial constitutional question . . . of importance to thousands of towns."

> *"If there is no conclusive evidence of the effectiveness of youth curfew laws, after decades of use, then there is no 'compelling state interest' necessary to deny young people their constitutional rights."*

There Is No Evidence That Juvenile Curfews Are Justified

Rich Jahn

In the following viewpoint Rich Jahn argues that juvenile curfew laws have been enacted hastily and are supported without proper consideration of the rights of young people. Jahn claims that juvenile curfews deny young people their constitutional rights and should be strongly supported by evidence that such laws reduce juvenile crime in order to be justified. Jahn recounts a study that doubts the effectiveness of juvenile curfew laws and claims there is no solid evidence in favor of the efficacy of curfews. As such, he concludes there is no good reason for the existence of juvenile curfews. Jahn is the member service director for the National Youth Rights Association (NYRA).

Criminalizing harmless behavior to prevent crime has long been the norm, particularly for young people, despite often, dubious evidence of its effectiveness. Many times people assume obvious correlations exist between youth behavior and social problems and remove their constitutional rights with the very minimal, or almost no evidence it is necessary. The most blatant example of this is the use of curfew laws, which have been challenged on a number of constitutional grounds. Despite their vast use across the nation over the last decade, no conclusive evidence can be amounted for their effectiveness in curtailing juvenile crime. Many communities have flaunted curfew laws as "great successes." However, no law enforcement agency has ever done any serious empirical study on curfew laws. Instead, evidence supporting curfews is mainly anecdotal and from survey data. Such data is problematic in that it focuses on perceived trends rather than actual trends. For example, while it is factual to claim [as Nicholas Riccardi does]:

> Monrovia, California's curfew adoption was followed by a 32 percent decline in residential burglaries.

One could also claim [as do Mike Males and Dan Macallair]:

> In 1992, San Francisco authorities dismantled their previously vigorous curfew enforcement, which had resulted in 1,400 arrests during the previous five years. Only three curfew arrests were made during 1993–97. Crime plummeted. From 1992 to 1997, juvenile murders declined fifty percent, property crimes reported to police declined thirty-six percent, and violent crimes reported to police declined by forty-one percent, the latter of which was the largest crime decrease of any large California city.

One may conclude from the first that curfew laws are effective and conclude from the second that they are not effective. However, neither is comparing the data to other controlled data sets, and so neither is adequately testing the hypothesis that curfew laws reduce juvenile crime. Nevertheless, the sheer amount of anecdotal data cannot be completely discounted. Most law enforcement officials in communities with curfews report they have perceived a decrease in juvenile crime since the institution of their curfews.

Curfews and Constitutional Rights

Curfew laws have been challenged on a variety of constitutional grounds. Although some may argue juveniles do not have constitutional rights, the Supreme Court in many cases has ruled that people have constitutional rights regardless of age. Often these cases have involved issues of students' rights in schools. *Tinker v. Des Moines School District* in 1969 ruled that students had the right to freedom of speech in schools. This case involved how school officials had forbidden a group of students from carrying out their symbolic protest of the Vietnam War by wearing black armbands. The constitutional rights of young people have been affirmed in many other cases, such as their religious freedom in schools, where religious activity is allowed as long as it is student led. In the case *Missouri v. Danforth* in 1976, it was directly stated that people have full constitutional rights regardless of age. In the court's opinion:

> Constitutional rights do not mature and come into being magically only when one attains the state-defined age of majority.

Although young people are subject to a large number of restrictions based upon age, the judicial system has a long precedent for people having full constitutional rights regardless of age.

The Supreme Court has long recognized that the rights of freedom of speech and assembly go hand in hand. In order to voice opinion, it is sometimes necessary to gather protests, and the only way to accomplish this is if there is freedom to gather in public as long as it is peaceful. The Fourteenth Amendment also guarantees that state and local governments cannot take away First Amendment rights. Many curfew laws, however, have exceptions written in them that allow offenders to be exempt if they are involved in a political protest. The importance of the use of public property such as streets and parks for conducting political speech has been protected by freedom of assembly under the First Amendment since *Hague v. CIO* in 1939. This case involved a group of people denied permits from the police for holding a meeting in a building in Jersey City for allegedly being communist. The city ordinance required anyone conducting a speech advocating obstruction of government to obtain a permit through the police station before getting a lease to any hall or building for conducting the speech. However, in *Cox v. Louisiana* (1965), it was ruled states may impose reasonable regulations upon assembly. In the opinion of the court:

> One would not be justified in ignoring the familiar red light because this was thought to be a means of social protest. Nor could one, contrary to traffic regulations, insist upon a street meeting in the middle of Times Square at the rush hour as a form of freedom of speech or assembly.

However, the regulatory measures must be narrowly defined to reach only the legitimate objectives of the state regulation. While the Supreme Court's interpretation of freedom of speech is broad, its interpretation of freedom of assembly appears to be narrow.

Curfews in the Courts

Curfew laws directly remove the right to assemble in public, and many times even on private property. The constitutionality of youth curfew laws has yet to be tested in the Supreme Court. Lower courts are divided over the issue, many ruling unconstitutional, and many ruling constitutional. The Supreme Court has only ever had one case to do with a curfew law in history, *Kiyoshi Hirabayashi v. United States* in 1943. This case was concerning the curfew imposed upon Japanese during World War II. It was upheld because the court felt constitutional rights were less applicable in times of war.

General curfews have often been imposed as a response to an emergency, such as riots, and they usually were implemented only a few days to a few weeks. The key difference is that they are intended from the start to be temporary, whereas youth curfews are intended to be permanent. A general curfew, which applied to all citizens to respond to a temporary emergency, was appealed to the Supreme Court in *Janet Stotland v. Commonwealth of Pennsylvania* [1970]. They refused to hear the case. However, Justice [William O.] Douglas dissented arguing that curfew laws may be necessary when the security of the state is threatened, but they raised serious questions about the right of assembly. He stated he was concerned about the possible abuse of curfew laws in clearing the public of "undesirable people," such as minorities, and he argued a curfew law should be temporary and narrowly defined.

The judicial system often applies a test to see if a law is narrowly defined enough and does not give the authorities too much power. Many lower courts that ruled a youth curfew law unconstitutional later ruled it constitutional after many exceptions were added into the law. Although curfew laws violate constitutional rights, the court's ruling in favor of curfew laws state they have a "compelling state interest" of reducing juvenile crime and victimization. Few people care about the rights of other people, and usually they only care about their own. Many adults seem not care about the rights of young people at all, by making their mere presence illegal. A survey conducted by Wichita State University asking cities nationwide a variety of questions concerning curfew laws found no city that didn't have a curfew law specifying constitutional issues as a reason for not having it. For these reasons, the only aspect about curfew laws that may really matter is if they are necessary, and if they do in fact accomplish their stated goals of reducing juvenile crime and victimization. Thus having a "compelling state interest."

The Justification for Juvenile Curfews

Nationwide, the majority of cities with curfew laws claim they are great successes in reducing crime. In a survey done by the U.S. Conference of Mayors, it was found that the officials in 88% of the cities with curfew laws believed that they helped reduce juvenile crime. However, as reported by the *Los Angeles Times*, the

Miniature crosses with victims' photos are displayed to commemorate the ten-year anniversary of the Columbine High School shootings in Littleton, Colorado. School shootings are given as a reason why some communities favor instituting curfew laws. © Marc Piscotty/Getty Images.

survey "did not include a statistical analysis of the effect curfews have had on crime." In addition, I was only able to find one study of the effectiveness of curfew laws that did a statistical hypothesis test that the level of curfew enforcement is negatively correlated with the level of other crime. It was the only one to use the basic procedures of using controlled data and testing for statistical significance. Curfews have been around for a long time, and the crime statistics to study them are readily available. The fact that virtually no research has been done, while so many people are claiming curfew laws are great successes, seems very irresponsible, and should lend itself to skepticism. Although statistics are often used to deceive, they're often the only way of measuring the real world, if done properly. Law enforcement agencies that say they "observe" a decline in juvenile crime should explain exactly how they observe it. Law enforcement officials report whatever crime measure conveniently shows crime has decreased. For example, the Office of Juvenile Justice and Delinquency Prevention did a study of curfew laws in 1996 and used crime victimization in some cities, arrest figures in others, and arrest figures for only selected crimes in still others. It made no controlled comparisons, and so it is useless for research purposes.

The main stated reasons for curfew laws is reducing juvenile crime and victimization, but is this really the reason for curfew laws? Two studies done by the LAPD [Los Angeles Police Department] in 1998 each came to opposite conclusions: One that the curfew law in Los Angeles increased crime, and the other that the curfew law decreased crime. Both reports, however, came to the same conclusion: that the curfew law should remain because it was an "effective tool." This, and the unwillingness to prove the effectiveness of curfew laws using any formal statistical analysis, suggests there may be other motivations for curfew laws.

A Study on Curfew Effectiveness

Sociologist Michael Males, a professor at the University of California, and Dan Macallair, did a broad study of the effectiveness of curfew laws in California. The study is available online, and he discusses it in his book. Males reports several criminologists reviewed his study before it was published in 1998 in the *Western Criminology Review*. However, he does not cite these criminologists. Males analyzed arrest, reported crime, and mortality data from jurisdictions throughout California for years 1980 to 1997. Males analyzed the correlation between the number of curfew arrests and the number of juvenile arrests for other crimes among the 12 most populous counties in California. He compared the levels of different types of crime, such as violent, homicide, property, and arson. He compared juvenile crime rates among cities with increasing levels of curfew enforcement with cities with declining levels of curfew enforcement.

[Males] analyzed the crime on a statewide level and on a local level in two case studies. His first case study involved an analysis of the correlation of the curfew law enforcement in Monrovia,

CA with the juvenile crime data for Monrovia. His second case study also involved a comparison of the correlation between curfew law enforcement and juvenile crime data in two cities, San José and San Francisco. San Francisco had high levels of curfew enforcement in the '80s, cut back in the '90s, and then repealed its curfew law in 1995. San José did the opposite, increasing its level of curfew enforcement in the '90s. Males tested the hypothesis that the correlation between the level of curfew enforcement and the level of juvenile crime was negative, meaning that as the level of curfew enforcement rose, the level of juvenile crime should have decreased. His conclusion was that he found no correlation between the level of curfew enforcement and the level of juvenile crime, and in some instances, the correlation was actually positively related. This was true for both the measures of reported crime and arrest rates.

Males believes arrest rates are the best available measure of juvenile crime, because the age of the offender is directly known. However, arrest rates do have one inherent flaw. They are unable to measure crime history. For example, a juvenile who committed one crime and is arrested and an adult who committed forty crimes and is arrested are both recorded as having one arrest, and so all statistics carry the same weight no matter how many crimes the offender committed. Despite this flaw, however, Males feels arrest rates are a better crime measure than the only other available method, which is reported crime. The vast majority of reported crime never results in an arrest, and so the age of the offender is usually never known. According to the FBI [Federal Bureau of Investigation] Uniform Crime Reports in 1997, adults commit seventy-five to ninety percent of all reported crime, and so statistics measuring juvenile crime trends that use reported crime are heavily biased. Despite this fact, after Males concluded his study, many curfew law supporters argued arrest figures were not a reliable measure for juvenile crime trends. They argued this even though many used arrest figures originally to argue for curfew laws. In response to critics, Males redid his study using reported crime as the measure, and he came to the same conclusion. Males' analysis of curfew laws throughout the state of California, over the maximum time period reliable data was available for, found no conclusive evidence that a correlation existed between the level of curfew enforcement and the level of juvenile crime that was statistically significant.

Criticism of the Study

The Monrovia, CA Police Department published a report refuting Males' and Dan Macallair's study written by the Chief of Police. Chief of Police, Joseph Santoro, argues Dan Macallair is biased, because he works for the Home School Legal Defense Association, [which] is suing the city of Monrovia over its daytime curfew law. This may be true, that Dan Macallair and Males are not the most objective researchers over the matter. However, if law enforcement agencies want a curfew law merely because they believe it is an "effective tool" regardless of how it affects crime, as the Los Angeles Police Department did, then they can hardly be called objective researchers either. The Monrovia, CA Police Department refutation contends Males' and Dan Macallair's work is also questionable because they received the data directly from the Home School Legal Defense Association. Males and Macallair, however, claim they obtained the data from primary sources:

> Data on crime by offense type, age of arrestee, year, and county are taken directly from the California Department of Justice's Law Enforcement Information Center (LEIC), annually reported statewide in *Crime and Delinquency in California* and by county and city in *California Criminal Justice Profile* through 1995 and statewide and by county in their 1996 and 1997 updates.

Santoro claims Males and Macallair are wrong to claim crime has increased due to curfew laws by analyzing arrest data, because the number of arrests simply increased because of officers discovering already existing crime due to more contact with juveniles. This is probably true. Arrest figures might also increase for adults if officers stopped and questioned every single adult they came into contact with. However, Males' and Dan Macallair's conclusion is not that curfew laws increase the level of crime. Specifically, their claim is they found no significant correlation between the level of curfew enforcement and the number of juvenile arrests comparing many different jurisdictions throughout California. Santoro cites anecdotal data. He says:

> Contrary to the study, after three years, Monrovia's program has contributed to a 39% reduction in truancy and 29% reduction in crime during school hours, including the following crimes associated with truancy:
>
> Residential Burglary Down 32%. Bicycle Theft Down 94%.
>
> Vehicle Burglary Down 59%. Disturbances Down 30%.
>
> Petty Theft Down 16%. Grand Theft Auto Down 46%.

Problems with the Data

The problem with anecdotal data is that there are too many questions. What is used to measure crime in this instance? Reported crime or arrest data? If both are used at the same time, then the results are incompatible with each other. How do these rates compare to before the curfew was instituted? Since crime has been decreasing overall, then it is probably more important to know if crime rates decreased significantly faster after the curfew law was instituted. How do the reductions in crime compare to other cities with and without curfew laws? How do the reductions in crime compare to adults who are not subject to the curfew law? If there was a 29% reduction in juvenile crime during curfew hours, then how was the crime rate affected during non-curfew hours?

Santoro argues Dan Macallair places too little emphasis on survey data obtained from cities by the U.S. Conference of

LOCAL AZ Chandler Curfew Squad © Brian Fairrington, www.politicalcartoons.com.

Mayors. They did mention the study. However, it is clear already that the vast majority of public policy leaders support the use of curfew laws, and they place no emphasis on empirical research at all. This was exactly the reason *for* Males' and Dan Macallair's study.

Most of the reports I researched about curfew laws were specifically addressing matters of policy. As a matter of policy, the explanation for curfew laws is primarily an effort to decrease juvenile crime. However, I find no explanations as to why specifically targeting juvenile crime is more important than targeting adult crime. Juvenile crime rates have been declining regardless of the existence of curfew laws or no curfew laws. Moreover, juvenile crime makes up the lowest proportion of crime altogether, except for the elderly. The report done by Wichita State University even states recent school shootings such as at Littleton, CO as a reason given by some communities for instituting curfew laws. The report admits there is a vague connection, at best, between curfew laws and school shootings. The perception of rapidly increasing juvenile crime may simply be increased attention to it. Despite the vast amount of expert testimony in support of curfew laws, there is no empirical evidence curfew laws actually work.

If Mike Males and Dan Macallair are biased in their study, then why are law enforcement agencies, or any other institution, completely unwilling to examine their study and conduct similar empirical studies? I found very little concern in any of the reports I read for the ethical issues involved with curfew laws, except from the American Civil Liberties Union. The proper response to crime, including juvenile crime, is to arrest people suspected of criminal conduct, not to keep millions of innocent, law-abiding young people under house arrest. If there is no conclusive evidence of the effectiveness of youth curfew laws, after decades of use, then there is no "compelling state interest" necessary to deny young people their constitutional rights.

"*The Court has consistently disapproved governmental action imposing criminal sanctions or denying rights and privileges solely because of a citizen's association with an unpopular organization.*"

It Is Unconstitutional for Schools to Prohibit Particular Political Associations

The Supreme Court's Decision

Lewis F. Powell Jr.

In the following viewpoint Lewis F. Powell Jr., writing for the majority of the US Supreme Court, contends that it is unconstitutional for a college to not recognize a particular student political association because it disagrees with its philosophy or because it is concerned about activities it might undertake. Powell claims that the freedom of association stems from the freedoms of speech, assembly, and petition in the First Amendment, and that the associational rights of college students deserve protection. Although he notes that the freedom to associate does give a student association license to act against the rules of an educational institution, only a legitimate intent to violate the rules would be grounds for failing to recognize a student association. Powell was an associate justice of the Supreme Court from 1972 until 1987.

Lewis F. Powell Jr., Majority opinion, *Healy v. James*, US Supreme Court, v. 408, June 26, 1972. www.laws.findlaw.com. Copyright © 1972 by Findlaw, a Thomson Reuters business.

This case, arising out of a denial by a state college of official recognition to a group of students who desired to form a local chapter of Students for a Democratic Society (SDS), presents this Court with questions requiring the application of well-established First Amendment principles. While the factual background of this particular case raises these constitutional issues in a manner not heretofore passed on by the Court, and only infrequently presented to lower federal courts, our decision today is governed by existing precedent.

The First Amendment on College Campuses

As the case involves delicate issues concerning the academic community, we approach our task with special caution, recognizing the mutual interest of students, faculty members, and administrators in an environment free from disruptive interference with the educational process. We also are mindful of the equally significant interest in the widest latitude for free expression and debate consonant with the maintenance of order. Where these interests appear to compete, the First Amendment, made binding on the States by the Fourteenth Amendment, strikes the required balance.

We mention briefly at the outset the setting in 1969–1970. A climate of unrest prevailed on many college campuses in this country. There had been widespread civil disobedience on some campuses, accompanied by the seizure of buildings, vandalism, and arson. Some colleges had been shut down altogether, while at others files were looted and manuscripts destroyed. SDS chapters on some of those campuses had been a catalytic force during this period. Although the causes of campus disruption were many and complex, one of the prime consequences of such activities was the denial of the lawful exercise of First Amendment rights to the majority of students by the few. Indeed, many of the most cherished characteristics long associated with institutions of higher learning appeared to be endangered. Fortunately, with the passage of time, a calmer atmosphere and greater maturity now pervade our campuses. Yet, it was in this climate of earlier unrest that this case arose.

Petitioners are students attending Central Connecticut State College (CCSC), a state-supported institution of higher learning. In September 1969 they undertook to organize what they then referred to as a "local chapter" of SDS. Pursuant to procedures established by the College, petitioners filed a request for official recognition as a campus organization with the Student Affairs Committee, a committee composed of four students, three faculty members, and the Dean of Student Affairs. The request specified three purposes for the proposed organization's existence. It would provide "a forum of discussion and self-education for students developing an analysis of American society"; it would serve as "an agency for integrating thought with action so as to

Mark Rudd, president of Students for a Democratic Society (SDS), addresses students at Columbia University, May 3, 1968. The Supreme Court ruled in 1972 that it was unconstitutional for Central Connecticut State College not to recognize a local SDS chapter. © Hulton Archive/Getty Images.

bring about constructive changes"; and it would endeavor to provide "a coordinating body for relating the problems of left-ist students" with other interested groups on campus and in the community. The Committee, while satisfied that the statement of purposes was clear and unobjectionable on its face, exhibited concern over the relationship between the proposed local group and the National SDS organization. In response to inquiries, rep-resentatives of the proposed organization stated that they would not affiliate with any national organization and that their group would remain "completely independent."

The Committee Hearings

In response to other questions asked by Committee members concerning SDS' reputation for campus disruption, the appli-cants made the following statements, which proved significant during the later stages of these proceedings:

Q. How would you respond to issues of violence as other [SDS] chapters have?

A. Our action would have to be dependent upon each issue.

Q. Would you use any means possible?

A. No I can't say that; would not know until we know what the issues are.

. . .

Q. Could you envision the [SDS] interrupting a class?

A. Impossible for me to say.

With this information before it, the Committee requested an additional filing by the applicants, including a formal statement regarding affiliations. The amended application filed in response stated flatly that "CCSC Students for a Democratic Society are not under the dictates of any National organization." At a sec-ond hearing before the Student Affairs Committee, the question of relationship with the National organization was raised again. One of the organizers explained that the National SDS was divided into several "factional groups," that the national-local relationship was a loose one, and that the local organization accepted only "certain ideas" but not all of the National organization's aims and philosophies. By a vote of six to two the Committee ultimately approved the application and recommended to the President of the College, Dr. [Don] James, that the organization be accorded official recognition. In approving the application, the majority indicated that its decision was premised on the belief that varying viewpoints should be represented on campus and that since the Young Americans for Freedom, the Young Democrats, the Young Republicans, and the Liberal Party all enjoyed recognized status, a group should be available with which "left wing" students might identify. The majority also noted and relied on the organization's claim of independence. Finally, it admonished the organization that immediate suspension would be considered if the group's activities proved incompatible with the school's policies against interference with the privacy of other students or destruction of property. The two dissenting members based their reservation primarily on the lack of clarity regarding the organization's independence.

The Rejection of Recognition

Several days later, the President rejected the Committee's recommendation, and issued a statement indicating that petitioners' organization was not to be accorded the benefits of official campus recognition. . . . He found that the organization's philosophy was antithetical to the school's policies, and that the group's independence was doubtful. He concluded that approval should not be granted to any group that "openly repudiates" the College's dedication to academic freedom.

Denial of official recognition posed serious problems for the organization's existence and growth. Its members were deprived of the opportunity to place announcements regarding meetings, rallies, or other activities in the student newspaper; they were precluded from using various campus bulletin boards; and—most importantly—non-recognition barred them from using campus facilities for holding meetings. This latter disability was brought home to petitioners shortly after the President's announcement. Petitioners circulated a notice calling a meeting to discuss what further action should be taken in light of the group's official rejection. The members met at the coffee shop in the Student Center ("Devils' Den") but were disbanded on the President's order since non-recognized groups were not entitled to use such facilities.

Their efforts to gain recognition having proved ultimately unsuccessful, and having been made to feel the burden of non-recognition, petitioners resorted to the courts. . . .

The Freedom of Association

At the outset we note that state colleges and universities are not enclaves immune from the sweep of the First Amendment. "It can hardly be argued that either students or teachers shed their constitutional rights to freedom of speech or expression at the schoolhouse gate" [*Tinker v. Des Moines Independent School District* (1969)]. Of course, as Mr. Justice [Abe] Fortas made clear in *Tinker*, First Amendment rights must always be applied "in light of the special characteristics of the . . . environment" in the particular case. And, where state-operated educational institutions are involved, this Court has long recognized "the need for affirming the comprehensive authority of the States and of school officials, consistent with fundamental constitutional safeguards, to prescribe and control conduct in the schools." Yet, the precedents of this Court leave no room for the view that, because of the acknowledged need for order, First Amendment protections should apply with less force on college campuses than in the community at large. Quite to the contrary, "[t]he vigilant protection of constitutional freedoms is nowhere more vital than in the community of American schools" [*Shelton v. Tucker* (1960)].

The college classroom with its surrounding environs is peculiarly the "marketplace of ideas," and we break no new constitutional ground in reaffirming this Nation's dedication to safeguarding academic freedom.

Among the rights protected by the First Amendment is the right of individuals to associate to further their personal beliefs. While the freedom of association is not explicitly set out in the Amendment, it has long been held to be implicit in the freedoms of speech, assembly, and petition. There can be no doubt that denial of official recognition, without justification, to college organizations burdens or abridges that associational right. The primary impediment to free association flowing from non-recognition is the denial of use of campus facilities for meetings and other appropriate purposes. The practical effect of non-recognition was demonstrated in this case when, several days after the President's decision was announced, petitioners were not allowed to hold a meeting in the campus coffee shop because they were not an approved group.

Petitioners' associational interests also were circumscribed by the denial of the use of campus bulletin boards and the school newspaper. If an organization is to remain a viable entity in a campus community in which new students enter on a regular basis, it must possess the means of communicating with these students. Moreover, the organization's ability to participate in the intellectual give and take of campus debate, and to pursue its stated purposes, is limited by denial of access to the customary media for communicating with the administration, faculty members, and other students. Such impediments cannot be viewed as insubstantial. . . .

It is to be remembered that the effect of the College's denial of recognition was a form of prior restraint, denying to petitioners' organization the range of associational activities described above. While a college has a legitimate interest in preventing disruption on the campus, which under circumstances requiring the safeguarding of that interest may justify such restraint, a "heavy burden" rests on the college to demonstrate the appropriateness of that action.

Grounds for Denial of Recognition

These fundamental errors—discounting the existence of a cognizable First Amendment interest and misplacing the burden of proof—require that the [lower court's] judgments . . . be reversed. But we are unable to conclude that no basis exists upon which non-recognition might be appropriate. Indeed, based on a reasonable reading of the ambiguous facts of this case, there appears to be at least one potentially acceptable ground for a denial of recognition. Because of this ambiguous state of the record we conclude that the case should be remanded, and, in an effort to provide guidance to the lower courts upon reconsideration, it is appropriate to discuss the several bases of President James' decision. Four possible justifications for non-recognition, all closely related, might be derived from the record and his statements. Three of those grounds are inadequate to substantiate his decision; a fourth, however, has merit.

From the outset the controversy in this case has centered in large measure around the relationship, if any, between petitioners' group and the National SDS. The Student Affairs Committee meetings, as reflected in its minutes, focused considerable attention on this issue; the court-ordered hearing also was directed primarily to this question. Despite assurances from petitioners and their counsel that the local group was in fact independent of the National organization, it is evident that President James was significantly influenced by his apprehension that there was a connection. Aware of the fact that some SDS chapters had been associated with disruptive and violent campus activity, he apparently considered that affiliation itself was sufficient justification for denying recognition.

Although this precise issue has not come before the Court heretofore, the Court has consistently disapproved governmental action imposing criminal sanctions or denying rights and privileges solely because of a citizen's association with an unpopular organization. In these cases it has been established that "guilt by association alone, without [establishing] that an individual's association poses the threat feared by the government" [*United States v. Robel* (1967)], is an impermissible basis upon which to deny First Amendment rights. The government has the burden of establishing a knowing affiliation with an organization possessing unlawful aims and goals, and a specific intent to further those illegal aims.

Students for a Democratic Society, as conceded by the College and the lower courts, is loosely organized, having various factions and promoting a number of diverse social and political views, only some of which call for unlawful action. Not only did petitioners proclaim their complete independence from this organization, but they also indicated that they shared only some of the beliefs its leaders have expressed. On this record it is clear that the relationship was not an adequate ground for the denial of recognition.

Disagreement of Philosophy

Having concluded that petitioners were affiliated with, or at least retained an affinity for, National SDS, President James attributed what he believed to be the philosophy of that organization to the local group. He characterized the petitioning group as adhering to "some of the major tenets of the national organization," including a philosophy of violence and disruption. Understandably, he found that philosophy abhorrent. In an article signed by President James in an alumni periodical, and made a part of the record below, he announced his unwillingness to "sanction an organization that openly advocates the destruction of the very ideals and freedoms upon which the academic life is founded." He further emphasized that the petitioners' "philosophies" were "counter to the official policy of the college."

The mere disagreement of the President with the group's philosophy affords no reason to deny it recognition. As repugnant as these views may have been, especially to one with President James' responsibility, the mere expression of them would not justify the denial of First Amendment rights. Whether petitioners did in fact advocate a philosophy of "destruction" thus becomes immaterial. The College, acting here as the instrumentality of the State, may not restrict speech or association simply because it finds the views expressed by any group to be abhorrent. As Mr. Justice [Hugo] Black put it most simply and clearly:

> I do not believe that it can be too often repeated that the freedoms of speech, press, petition and assembly guaranteed by the First Amendment must be accorded to the ideas we hate or sooner or later they will be denied to the ideas we cherish [*Communist Party v. SACB* (dissenting opinion) (1961)].

Disruptive Activities

As the litigation progressed in the District Court, a third rationale for President James' decision—beyond the questions of affiliation and philosophy—began to emerge. His second statement, issued after the court-ordered hearing, indicates that he based rejection on a conclusion that this particular group would be a "disruptive influence at CCSC." This language was underscored in the second District Court opinion. In fact, the court concluded that the President had determined that CCSC-SDS' "prospective campus activities were likely to cause a disruptive influence at CCSC."

If this reason, directed at the organization's activities rather than its philosophy, were factually supported by the record, this Court's prior decisions would provide a basis for considering the propriety of non-recognition. The critical line heretofore drawn for determining the permissibility of regulation is the line between mere advocacy and advocacy "directed to inciting or producing imminent lawless action and . . . likely to incite or produce such action" [*Brandenburg v. Ohio* (1969)]. In the context of the "special characteristics of the school environment," the power of the government to prohibit "lawless action" is not limited to acts of a criminal nature. Also prohibitable are actions which "materially and substantially disrupt the work and discipline of the school" [*Tinker*]. Associational activities need not be tolerated where they infringe reasonable campus rules, interrupt classes, or substantially interfere with the opportunity of other students to obtain an education. . . .

There was no substantial evidence that these particular individuals acting together would constitute a disruptive force on campus. Therefore, insofar as non-recognition flowed from such fears, it constituted little more than the sort of "undifferentiated fear or apprehension of disturbance [which] is not enough to overcome the right to freedom of expression."

Reasonable Standards of Conduct

These same references in the record to the group's equivocation regarding how it might respond to "issues of violence" and whether it could ever "envision . . . interrupting a class," suggest a fourth possible reason why recognition might have been denied to these petitioners. These remarks might well have been read as announcing petitioners' unwillingness to be bound by reasonable school rules governing conduct. The College's Statement of Rights, Freedoms, and Responsibilities of Students contains, as we have seen, an explicit statement with respect to campus disruption. The regulation, carefully differentiating between advocacy and action, is a reasonable one, and petitioners have not questioned it directly. Yet their statements raise considerable question whether they intend to abide by the prohibitions contained therein. . . .

Just as in the community at large, reasonable regulations with respect to the time, the place, and the manner in which student groups conduct their speech-related activities must be respected. A college administration may impose a requirement, such as may have been imposed in this case, that a group seeking official recognition affirm in advance its willingness to ad-

The Freedom to Associate

Effective advocacy of both public and private points of view, particularly controversial ones, is undeniably enhanced by group association, as this Court has more than once recognized by remarking
upon the close nexus between the freedoms of speech and assembly. It is beyond debate that freedom to engage in association for
the advancement of beliefs and ideas is an inseparable aspect of
the "liberty" assured by the Due Process Clause of the Fourteenth
Amendment, which embraces freedom of speech. Of course, it is
immaterial whether the beliefs sought to be advanced by association pertain to political, economic, religious or cultural matters, and
state action which may have the effect of curtailing the freedom to
associate is subject to the closest scrutiny.

Marshall Harlan II, NAACP v. Alabama,
Majority opinion, June 30, 1958.

here to reasonable campus law. Such a requirement does not impose an impermissible condition on the students' associational
rights. Their freedom to speak out, to assemble, or to petition
for changes in school rules is in no sense infringed. It merely
constitutes an agreement to conform with reasonable standards
respecting conduct. This is a minimal requirement, in the interest of the entire academic community, of any group seeking the
privilege of official recognition. . . .

We think the above discussion establishes the appropriate
framework for consideration of petitioners' request for campus
recognition. Because respondents failed to accord due recognition to First Amendment principles, the judgments . . . approving
respondents' denial of recognition must be reversed. Since we
cannot conclude from this record that petitioners were willing to
abide by reasonable campus rules and regulations, we order the
case remanded for reconsideration. We note, in so holding, that

the wide latitude accorded by the Constitution to the freedoms of expression and association is not without its costs in terms of the risk to the maintenance of civility and an ordered society. Indeed, this latitude often has resulted, on the campus and elsewhere, in the infringement of the rights of others. Though we deplore the tendency of some to abuse the very constitutional privileges they invoke, and although the infringement of rights of others certainly should not be tolerated, we reaffirm this Court's dedication to the principles of the Bill of Rights upon which our vigorous and free society is founded.

"Advocating for free speech is a perfect opportunity to establish a fraternity as an 'expressive association.'"

Student Fraternities Can Be Protected as Expressive Associations

Greg Lukianoff and Matthew Vasconcellos

In the following viewpoint Greg Lukianoff and Matthew Vasconcellos argue that free speech on college campuses is under assault. Lukianoff and Vasconcellos contend that fraternities can benefit themselves and the campus community by advocating free speech as one of their causes. One of the benefits to fraternities, they claim, is the benefit of being viewed as an expressive association under the law, granting greater protection for speech its members make. The authors conclude that it is important for fraternities to stand up for their First Amendment rights in order to protect free speech for all. Lukianoff is the president of the Foundation for Individual Rights in Education (FIRE) and Vasconcellos is an attorney in Chicago.

I. Introduction

While there is no shortage of free speech battles on college campuses, fraternities have the dubious honor of being at the center of many of the least sympathetic controversies. From Halloween parties where brothers show up dressed as Ku Klux Klan members to fraternity newsletters that graphically relate a brother's sexual exploits with named co-eds, fraternities sometimes express themselves in ways that are not exactly likely to win the battle for hearts and minds. However, although fraternities may later regret the actions of some of their brothers, they must not allow their rights to be stripped away by overzealous or opportunistic administrators. The freedoms of all college and university students may rest on fraternities' willingness to stand up for their rights.[1]

The following piece is not primarily a legal article. Rather, it focuses on practical advice the Foundation for Individual Rights in Education (FIRE) can offer after years of fighting for free speech on campus. Based on FIRE's observation that fraternities repeatedly make the same kinds of mistakes, this article is an effort to guide fraternities on what to do when a free speech controversy arises. It is also an effort to recruit fraternities for a war that so many have found themselves drafted into unwillingly: the ongoing war for free speech on campus.

II. Tips on how to be prepared for a free speech battle with a university

1. Remember that assaults on fraternities' right of free speech are part of a larger problem on campus.

Fraternities are by no means alone in having their rights abridged. A quick examination of FIRE's website (www.thefire.org) or the Student Press Law Center (www.splc.org) demonstrates the pervasiveness of assaults on free speech on campus. Many of these controversies are downright absurd, such as Gonzaga University's decision to punish the College Republicans for "discriminatory" language after they used the word "hate" on a flyer advertising a lecture by author Daniel J. Flynn, whose recent book was entitled "Why the Left Hates America"; or Texas Tech University's establishment of a "speech zone" that restricted free expression for the University's 28,000 students to one 20-foot-wide "Free Speech Gazebo." These cases, along with dozens of others, demonstrate that many universities are not, even minimally, living up to the ideals of truly open and free-flowing expression on which an intellectually robust university depends.

2. Stand up for free speech on campus, even when your fraternity is not in trouble.

Free speech is too often taken for granted until an organization faces a challenge to its own existence. Beyond the obvious good of defending one of our country's deepest principles, a fraternity advocating free speech as one of its causes achieves additional benefits both for the fraternity and for the university as a whole.

Conservative students at the University of California hold an "affirmative action bake sale." The authors of this viewpoint argue that such protests are a fully protected form of political satire and not discrimination in any legal sense. © AP Photo/Marcio Jose Sanchez.

First, it provides an opportunity to educate brothers about free speech, its parameters, its limits, and common controversies that have arisen. At the same time, it provides an opportunity to remind brothers that the *right* to engage in a particular form of expression does not make that expression *wise* or *good*. Although "offensive" expression is protected by the First Amendment, brothers will learn from accounts of previous fraternity speech controversies that it may subject a fraternity to unwanted public scorn or embarrassment. These lessons may help prevent potentially troublesome situations in the future.

Second, successfully defending against an attack on the free speech rights of other groups may prevent administrators from attempting to use similar tactics in the future. For example, in 2003, the University of California at Irvine shut down the College Republicans' "affirmative action bake sale"—a widely-used political protest parodying affirmative action policies—arguing that it was a form of "discrimination." Regardless of what one thinks about the propriety of such protests, the "bake sale" was a fully-protected form of political satire and not "discrimination" in any legal sense. FIRE intervened by writing to the university and explaining why UCI's actions violated both the letter and spirit of the First Amendment and bringing the case national media attention. A few months after FIRE's intervention, the College Republicans held the sale again, and instead of official repression, the bake sale was allowed to proceed without administrative intervention. After a brief and public outcry against its actions, UCI learned it could not use "discrimination" as a back door to censorship. By intervening in such free speech controversies, fraternities can educate their university that commonly-used tactics to circumvent free speech rights will not be quietly tolerated. In this way, taking such action may prevent attempts to silence speech in the future.

Third, standing up for others' rights may mean that the fraternity will not be alone if or when it needs defending. A fraternity that supports a university's decision to punish the expression of another group will not have a great deal of support when its own rights are challenged. While, legally, the popularity of a particular expression is irrelevant to its protected status, as a practical matter, the support of other groups or the student media can prevent a free speech controversy from mushrooming into a witch-hunt.

Finally, and perhaps most importantly from a legal standpoint, speaking out on such issues may have an additional surprising benefit: it may help secure a chapter's legal position as an expressive association in the future. A recent federal appeals court ruling, *Pi Lambda Phi Fraternity, Inc. v. University of Pittsburgh*, 229 F.3d 435 (3rd Cir., 2000), held that fraternities that speak out on issues are more likely to be entitled to free association protection than those that do not. In that case, the Third Circuit denied a fraternity the protections afforded to "expressive associations" stating: "Nothing in the record indicates that the Chapter ever took a public stance on any issue of public political, social, or cultural importance" *Id* at 444. If ever your right to exist on campus is challenged, your position will be greatly enhanced if you have previously taken positions on issues and actively exercised your right to speak. Advocating for free speech is a perfect opportunity to establish your fraternity as an "expressive association."

III. What to do when a free speech controversy arises

1. When a free speech incident takes place, get organized.

First, get the facts straight. Controversial events often lead to emotionally charged and heated debates that may distort the reality of the incident; thus, establishing and publicizing the facts of what happened before the truth gets obscured by rhetoric are both extremely important. At Georgia State University in 2003, several members of Pi Kappa Alpha painted their faces black for a hip-hop–themed Halloween party for which they dressed as rappers Snoop Dogg and Chingy. According to reports, when other members of the fraternity saw the students, they advised the brothers to remove the paint and the students complied. However, the brothers and the fraternity were punished after fellow students reported the incident to the administration.

During the debate that followed, a group pressing for the fraternity's removal produced flyers featuring a photograph of another "blackface" incident at Auburn University where a fraternity brother was shown in a Ku Klux Klan robe simulating a lynching of another brother in blackface. The flyers wrongfully implied that the photograph depicted members of Pi Kappa Alpha. With no other information, a student looking at such a flyer would likely accept it as authoritative. However, an honest, early and comprehensive accounting of what took place could preempt such distortions and provide a fraternity with the opportunity to present facts that may paint its actions in a less harmful light. In the GSU case, for example, the fraternity took responsible action and asked the brothers to take off the offensive paint. Facts like these have no bearing on the legal right of the brothers to wear a provocative Halloween costume, but may help convince some students or some administrators to not escalate the situation.

When an incident occurs, a fraternity should conduct a thorough investigation to get as complete a picture of what happened as possible. When it has a reliable set of facts, the group should publicize them in various media. Letters should be written to the campus or local newspaper, the administration, other campus groups, the national organization and alumni. The account should be honest and should not try to hide unpleasant facts. If the group regrets any actions taken by it or its brothers, it may apologize to the offended party; however, the group must also make clear that it remains united and willing to fight any sanctions.

As a note of caution, in our experience, an apology often has little or no effect on the determination of those who wish to see a fraternity disciplined, so one should not expect that even the most contrite statement of regret will make the controversy go away. While apologies are appropriate if the fraternity regrets the actions of its brothers, it is more important to prepare for the upcoming contest by establishing the record and staking its position as soon as possible. If it still looks like a fraternity will be punished once it has taken the above actions, it should submit the case to FIRE at www.thefire.org.

2. Do not accept punishment when the expression in question is protected by the First Amendment.

Once the administration takes action, the fraternity needs to decide how it will respond. It is essential that fraternities not accept illegitimate excuses to punish the content of their expression. The most common approach universities have taken to justify assaults on protected expression is by portraying such expression as a form of "discriminatory harassment" that the university is required to prevent under federal law. Discriminatory harassment is a very specific legal category of punishable conduct that attempts to ensure that all students are provided with access to educational opportunities. It does *not* give a university the right to prohibit merely "offensive" speech, as often claimed.[2] Abuse of "discriminatory harassment" has been so rampant that, in July 2003, the Department of Education's Office of Civil Rights (OCR) felt it necessary to release a clarification on the law to universities, explaining that:

> [I]n addressing harassment allegations, OCR has recognized that the offensiveness of a particular expression, standing alone, is not a legally sufficient basis to establish a hostile environment under the statutes enforced by OCR. . . . Some colleges and universities have interpreted OCR's prohibition of "harassment" as encompassing all offensive speech regarding sex, disability, race or other classifications. Harassment, however, to be prohibited by the statutes within OCR's jurisdiction, must include something beyond the mere expression of views, words, symbols or thoughts that some person finds offensive.

Any accusation against a fraternity for "discriminatory harassment" as defined by Title IX simply because students found a brother's expression "offensive" is an illegitimate use of federal law and, for the sake of the fraternity and other groups on campus, any punishment based on such a regulation should be rejected.

In addition to the clear statement from OCR, numerous court decisions have enshrined in law what OCR has articulated as policy: that student expression cannot be prohibited or punished as "discriminatory" because it is offensive to other members of the university. The leading case of fraternal speech, *IOTA XI Chapter of Sigma Chi Fraternity v. George Mason University*, 993 F.2d 386 (4th Cir., 1993), overturned the punishment, under the university's anti-discrimination policy, of a fraternity that held an "ugly woman contest" in which fraternity members dressed as various offensive and insulting racial- and gender-based caricatures. While the court recognized that a university has a "substantial interest in maintaining an educational environment free of discrimination and racism," it concluded that "the university should have accomplished its goals in some fashion other than silencing speech on the basis of viewpoint" *Id* at 393. Another federal court struck down the University of Michigan's "Policy on Discrimination and Discriminatory Harassment of Students in the University Environment," holding that "what the University could not do . . . was establish an anti-discrimination policy which had the effect of prohibiting certain speech because it disagreed with ideas or messages sought to be conveyed" *Doe v. University of Michigan*, 721 F. Supp. 852, 864 (Dist. E.D. Mich, 1989), *see also Dambrot v. Central Mich. Univ.*, 55 F.3d 1177 (6th Cir. 1995); *The UWM Post, Inc. v. Board of Regents of University of Wisconsin System* 774 F. Supp. 1163 (E.D. Wisc. 1991); Harvey A. Silverglate and Greg Lukianoff, *Speech Codes: Alive and Well at Colleges*, Chronicle of Higher Education, Aug. 1, 2003 at 7. Policies against "harassment" cannot be used to punish students or organizations, fraternities included, based on the message they convey—even if the message is offensive, crude, insulting, or, indeed, genuinely racist or sexist.

3. Be willing to fight for free speech: you will likely win.

In FIRE's experience, whether due to a reluctance to defend some of the actions of their brothers. a desire to avoid a confrontation with the administration, or a basic misunderstanding of their rights, fraternities too often do not fight back when universities impose punishment for engaging in protected speech. However, fraternities, their alumni, and their nationals must remember that in our legal system, all citizens only enjoy the rights that the least of us enjoy. Therefore, fraternities need to realize that what might seem like a trivial fight over an offensive Halloween costume may have a profound impact on administrators' or students' approaches to dealing with speech in the future.

Fraternities willing to fight for their free speech rights usually prevail. Universities have come to depend on the acquiescence of students when they impose illegitimate sanctions for protected speech. When challenged, however, pressure from the public, the media, alumni, donors, and organizations like FIRE is often enough to force a university to back away from morally and constitutionally objectionable sanctions against students or organizations. When public pressure does not suffice, lawsuits usually do.

In those rare instances where a university has insisted on litigating such cases, they typically lose. The cases cited above are somewhat rare examples of fully-litigated cases involving free speech rights of students. Often when a fraternity or other organization files a lawsuit, the university backs down shortly thereafter. For example, when officials at the University of California Riverside disbanded a chapter of Phi Kappa Sigma for three years after it produced a t-shirt that some Latino students found offensive, the fraternity filed suit. The university quickly reversed the sanctions, settled the lawsuit, and agreed to have two top administrators attend First Amendment "sensitivity training."

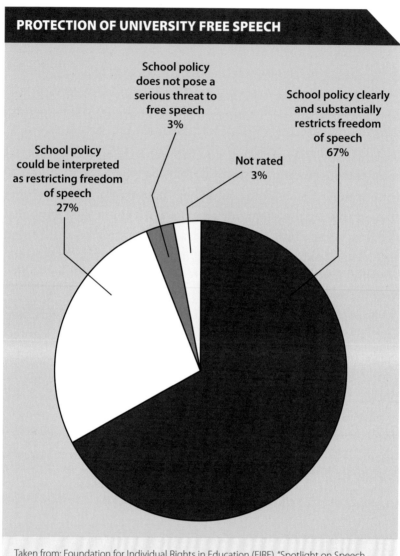

PROTECTION OF UNIVERSITY FREE SPEECH

School policy does not pose a serious threat to free speech
3%

School policy could be interpreted as restricting freedom of speech
27%

Not rated
3%

School policy clearly and substantially restricts freedom of speech
67%

Taken from: Foundation for Individual Rights in Education (FIRE), "Spotlight on Speech Codes 2011: The State of Free Speech on Our Nation's Campuses," December 20, 2010.

Similar scenarios involving fraternities have occurred at Auburn University and Cal State Northridge. When the fraternities filed lawsuits alleging a violation of their free speech rights, the universities readmitted the chapters and settled the lawsuits. Given the clear weight of the law against such unconstitutional policies, one can easily see why universities are so reluctant to take their cases to court.

IV. Conclusion

We have not seen the last time a fraternity gets in trouble for offensive expression, but FIRE hopes that the next time such a controversy arises, the fraternity, its alumni, and national governing body will recognize the importance of protecting the right to free speech. Standing up for free speech in general does not mean the same thing as endorsing the expression itself. Defending expression that is unpopular or that one disagrees with personally requires courage and principle, and is crucial to safeguarding the rights of all students. We hope that by following the advice briefly outlined in this article, fraternities may move away from being the poster children for those who support speech codes, to being positive allies in the fight for free speech.

Notes

1. A note of caution: some of the analysis that follows concerns primarily fraternities at public colleges and universities. Private schools have greater latitude to restrict otherwise constitutional rights of students. However, students at private schools that claim to value free speech can and should insist on their *moral* right to free speech, even if their legal rights are in question. Furthermore, private schools also use Title IX's anti-discrimination clauses as an excuse to punish student speech so the analysis of Title IX applies equally to public and private universities.

2. The only Supreme Court case that has dealt with student-on-student harassment defined "harassment" as a pattern of behavior "so severe, pervasive, and objectively offensive that it can be said to deprive the victims of access to the educational opportunities or benefits provided by the school" *Davis v. Monroe County Board of Education.* 526 U.S. 629, 650-651 (1999). In that case, which concerned grade schoolers, the behavior in question included physical and sexual assault.

> "Based on its size, level of selectivity,
> purpose, and inclusion of non-
> members, the Fraternity lacks the
> characteristics that typify groups with
> strong claims to intimate association."

A School Policy Restricting an All-Male Fraternity Does Not Violate Freedom of Association

The Circuit Court's Decision

Pierre Leval

In the following viewpoint Pierre Leval, writing for the US Court of Appeals for the Second Circuit, contends that it does not violate students' rights to freedom of association if a college chooses to only recognize social clubs that are open to all students. Leval claims that the constitutional right to freedom of association protects only intimate association and that the all-male fraternity at issue in this case does not qualify for heightened protection of their association. As such, Leval concludes that the college's non-discrimination policy justifies the college's refusal to recognize the all-male fraternity at the college. Leval is a judge for the US Court of Appeals for the Second Circuit, appointed by President Bill Clinton in 1993.

Pierre Leval, Majority opinion, *Chi Iota Colony of Alpha Epsilon Pi Fraternity v. City University of New York*, US Court of Appeals for the Second Circuit, v. 502, September 13, 2007. www.ca2.uscourts.gov. Copyright © 2007 by US Court of Appeals.

This is an appeal by the defendant City University of New York, a public university, from a preliminary injunction imposed by the United States District Court for the Eastern District of New York barring the university's constituent, the College of Staten Island ("CSI"), from enforcing against the plaintiff fraternity, Chi Iota Colony ("the Fraternity"), a non-discrimination policy, which restricts official recognition of a student group to those that do not discriminate on the basis of gender.

The Lower Court's Decision

The Fraternity asserted a right of associative freedom under the First Amendment to limit its membership to male students and contended that CSI's withholding of recognition (and the benefits thereof) by reason of the Fraternity's discriminatory membership policy constituted infringement of a constitutionally guaranteed right. According to the district court's analysis, the crucial question was whether the interest claimed by the Fraternity in single-sex membership was recognized by the First Amendment. Upon concluding that the interest was so recognized, the court reasoned that CSI's contrary policy must be judged under a strict scrutiny test, which the policy could not survive.

As explained below, we believe the district court applied the wrong test and, as a result, reached an incorrect conclusion. The mere fact that the associational interest asserted is recognized by the First Amendment does not necessarily mean that a regulation which burdens that interest must satisfy strict scrutiny. In assessing a First Amendment associational-rights claim, a court must balance the associational interest asserted against the conflicting regulatory interest.

In this case, at least upon the record established for purposes of a preliminary injunction, we conclude that the balance of interests favors CSI, and therefore the school is entitled to enforce its non-discriminatory policy against the Fraternity. We therefore reverse the district court's grant of a preliminary injunction.

The College's Non-Discrimination Policy

The College of Staten Island is a public college within the City University of New York system. As of 2004, CSI had about 11,000 undergraduates, 40% of whom were male. CSI is committed to pluralism and diversity. The school's mission statement says that it hopes to instill in its students "a sensitivity to pluralism and diversity," and that it views "[e]fforts to promote diversity and to combat bigotry [as] an inextricable part of [its] educational mission." The school requires all students to fulfill a "Pluralism and Diversity" requirement by taking at least one course on that topic; CSI also has a policy of "provid[ing] services for students without regard to . . . sex."

CSI encourages students to form clubs in order to "support, enrich, extend, and amplify the goals of CSI's educational mission." In order to be officially recognized and to qualify for various benefits, "the purpose and goals of the student organization must exhibit a clear relationship with the educational mission of [CSI] by demonstrating a commitment to one or more" enumerated objectives. The list of enumerated objectives includes general values such as "promotion of service," "spiritual growth and development," and "promotion and development of cultural diversity and awareness."

In order for a student group to gain recognition, it must comply with CSI's non-discrimination policy:

> [M]embership and participation in it must be available to all eligible students of the College. In addition, in order to be recognized, each organization must agree not to discriminate on the basis of . . . gender. . . .

The Male Fraternity

Chi Iota Colony is a male, social fraternity, which draws its members primarily from the CSI student body. As of September 2005, the Fraternity had eighteen members who were CSI students and

Relationships Deserving Constitutional Protection

The Court has long recognized that, because the Bill of Rights is designed to secure individual liberty, it must afford the formation and preservation of certain kinds of highly personal relationships a substantial measure of sanctuary from unjustified interference by the State. . . .

Family relationships, by their nature, involve deep attachments and commitments to the necessarily few other individuals with whom one shares not only a special community of thoughts, experiences, and beliefs, but also distinctively personal aspects of one's life. Among other things, therefore, they are distinguished by such attributes as relative smallness, a high degree of selectivity in decisions to begin and maintain the affiliation, and seclusion from others in critical aspects of the relationship. As a general matter, only relationships with these sorts of qualities are likely to reflect the considerations that have led to an understanding of freedom of association as an intrinsic element of personal liberty. Conversely, an association lacking these qualities—such as a large business enterprise—seems remote from the concerns giving rise to this constitutional protection. . . .

Between these poles, of course, lies a broad range of human relationships that may make greater or lesser claims to constitutional protection from particular incursions by the State. Determining the limits of state authority over an individual's freedom to enter into a particular association therefore unavoidably entails a careful assessment of where that relationship's objective characteristics locate it on a spectrum from the most intimate to the most attenuated of personal attachments.

William J. Brennan Jr., Majority opinion,
Roberts v. United States Jaycees, *US Supreme Court, July 3, 1984.*

one member who was not. The Fraternity has placed no limit on its size but has never before exceeded twenty members.

The Fraternity identifies itself as a Jewish organization devoted to "the inculcation of the traditional values of men's college social fraternities . . . community service, and the expression of Jewish culture." Its charter states that the group aims "[t]o foster and promote brotherly love, to inaugurate a spirit of cooperation and helpfulness . . . [and] to encourage vigorous participation in university, college and general activities in [the] community. . . ." Though most Fraternity members are non-practicing Jews, the group welcomes non-Jewish members, and several current members are not Jewish.

The Fraternity does not admit women. According to its president, "The selective, single-sex, all-male nature of the Fraternity is essential to achieving and maintaining the congeniality, cohesion and stability that enable it to function as a surrogate family and to meet [the] social, emotional and cultural needs of its members." He explained that admitting women might lead to romantic relationships between members, causing "inevitable jealousies and other conflicts." Even admitting lesbians might disrupt the special bonds between Fraternity members, because "[h]aving a female in the fraternity is an issue itself." . . .

The Right to Intimate Association

The right to intimate association protects the close ties between individuals from inappropriate interference by the power of the state. To determine whether a governmental rule unconstitutionally infringes on an associational freedom, courts balance the strength of the associational interest in resisting governmental interference with the state's justification for the interference. This will require an assessment of: (1) the strength of the associational interests asserted and their importance to the plaintiff; (2) the degree to which the rule interferes with those interests; (3) the public interests or policies served by the rule imposed; and (4) the tailoring of the rule to effectuate those interests or policies. The more important the associational interest asserted, and the more the challenged governmental rule burdens the associational freedom, the more persuasive must be the state's reasons for the intrusion, and the more precisely tailored the state's policy must be.

Where a policy interferes with core associational liberties, "it cannot be upheld unless it is supported by sufficiently important state interests and is closely tailored to effectuate only those interests" [*Zablocki* v. *Redhail* (1978)]. For instance, where a governmental regulation substantially interferes with close familial relationships, the most exigent level of inquiry—strict scrutiny— is applied. By contrast, where the associational interest claimed by the plaintiff is of less importance, and where the regulation challenged interferes only minimally with the associational freedom, the state's justification for the regulation need not be as weighty. . . .

The Strength of the Associational Interest

The right to intimate association "reflects the realization that individuals draw much of their emotional enrichment from close ties with others," ties that allow for the cultivation and transmittal of shared beliefs. The relationships that have been afforded the most vigorous protection include those involved in the "creation and sustenance of a family"—namely marriage, the begetting, raising, and education of children, and cohabitation with relatives. The Supreme Court has explained that these relationships "exemplify" what the right to intimate association is meant to protect, and the Court has cautioned that such relationships "suggest some relevant limitations on the relationships that might be entitled to . . . constitutional protection" [*Roberts v. US Jaycees* (1984)]. However, the Court has declined to restrict the right to intimate association to the family context. Instead of adopting a categorical approach, the Court has instructed that relationships must be "locate[d] . . . on a spectrum from the most intimate to the most attenuated of personal attachments" [*Bd. of Dirs. of Rotary Int'l* v. *Rotary Club of Duarte* (1987)]. Criteria used to measure the strength of an association's interest in intimacy include "size, purpose, selectivity, and whether others are excluded from critical aspects of the relationship." We examine these particulars in the context of the Fraternity's claim.

Size The Fraternity currently has nineteen members, eighteen of whom are CSI students and one of whom is not. It aspires to one day have about fifty pledges per semester. But the Fraternity places no limit on membership size. The fact that the membership roll is not larger is due to the fact that CSI is primarily a commuter campus. Thus, the size limitation is the product of circumstances, not a desire to maintain intimacy. These characteristics render the Fraternity similar to other groups whose intimate-association interests were held to be weak.

Selectivity The Fraternity employs some care in selecting recruits in order to ensure that all its members are compatible. Every prospective member goes through a screening interview that involves personal questions, and decisions about whom to invite are made in consultation with all current members.

However, upon each year's graduation, the Fraternity presumably ceases to associate regularly with a quarter of its members and seeks to replace them with new members. Like the Rotary Clubs in *Duarte*, the Fraternity must "keep a flow of prospects coming to make up for . . . attrition and gradually to enlarge the membership." The Fraternity thus aggressively recruits new members from the CSI student body. Fraternity members invite approximately one out of ten men they meet on campus—and about a third of the men they know through Jewish groups—to rush events. Most of those who attend a first rush event are invited back for later events, and the majority of those who attend multiple events are asked to pledge. Most, though not all, pledges are initiated as members. These figures indicate that a relatively high percentage of Jewish men at CSI who express an interest in the Fraternity are invited to join. The degree of selectivity displayed by the Fraternity in choosing new members thus compares unfavorably with that employed in creating the strongest of associational interests, as in the cases of marriage or adoption.

Purpose The Fraternity's purposes are generally inclusive. The Fraternity aims to "foster and promote brotherly love, to inaugurate a spirit of cooperation and helpfulness . . . [and] to encourage vigorous participation in university, college and general activities in [the] community . . . ." The Fraternity hopes to promote in its members a respect for "the traditional values of men's college social fraternities . . . community service, and the expression of Jewish culture." These are broad, public-minded goals that do not depend for their promotion on close-knit bonds.

To be sure, the Fraternity also seeks to foster personal, intimate relationships between its members. According to its president, Fraternity brothers form "deep attachments and commitments" and share "a community of thoughts, experiences, beliefs and distinctly personal aspects of their lives." But the same can be said of nearly any student group in which members become close friends. As the Supreme Court explained in rejecting a facial challenge to an anti-discrimination law that affected clubs with more than 400 members:

> It may well be that a considerable amount of private or intimate association occurs in such a setting, as is also true in many restaurants and other places of public accommodation, but that fact alone does not afford the entity as a whole any constitutional immunity to practice discrimination when the government has barred it from doing so [*N.Y. State Club Ass'n, Inc. v. City of N.Y.* (1988)].

Exclusion of Non-Members It is true that some Fraternity activities take place only among its members. Decisions about whether to offer or revoke membership occur in private, as do the ceremonies in which prospective members become pledges and pledges become full members. Weekly business meetings and frequent informal gatherings also take place only in the presence of members.

Nonetheless, the Fraternity involves non-members in several crucial aspects of its existence. Many rush events are held in public places such as local cafés or pool halls. During its February 2003 rush, the Fraternity planned several events requiring the interaction of current and prospective members with non-members—a party, as well as outings to a strip club, a karaoke bar, and a laser

The ruling in this viewpoint contends that schools do not violate students' rights to freedom of association if they choose not to recognize social clubs, such as all-male fraternities, that are not open to all students. © AP Photo/Lake Superior State University, Lance Boehmer.

tag establishment. Once they join, many Fraternity members attend public weekly meetings with the JAM [Jewish Awareness Movement] and a rabbi. The Fraternity also participates with the JAM in other Jewish-themed events. The Fraternity gives parties, sometimes at a profit, at which non-members—including women—are encouraged to attend. Social events involving non-members occur "perhaps once or twice a month." . . .

Based on its size, level of selectivity, purpose, and inclusion of non-members, the Fraternity lacks the characteristics that typify groups with strong claims to intimate association.

Also important is the fact that CSI's non-discrimination policy interferes only to a limited extent with the Fraternity's associational rights. CSI's policy does not prevent the Fraternity from continuing to exist, to hold intimate meetings, to exclude women, or to exercise selectivity in choosing new members. Denial of recognition has consequences primarily for the Fraternity's non-intimate aspects. CSI's denial of use of school facilities interferes more with the Fraternity's ability to solicit strangers from future classes to become new members than it interferes with the ability of its existing members to gather and share intimate associations. The Fraternity has not shown that the unavailability of school facilities makes it impossible, or even difficult, to find suitable places for meetings. CSI's refusal to subsidize the Fraternity's activities does not constitute a substantial imposition on the group's associational freedom.

The State's Interest

CSI's interests in applying its non-discrimination policy are substantial. As the district court acknowledged, "[t]here is undoubtedly a compelling interest in eradicating discrimination based on gender." The school's mission statement declares that "[e]fforts to promote diversity and to combat bigotry . . . are an inextricable part of the educational mission of the University." CSI encourages students to form clubs in order to support the school's goals. To gain recognition, a club must "exhibit a clear relationship with the educational mission" of CSI. By denying recognition to student groups that reject members based on gender, CSI's anti-discrimination policy directly promotes the significant, consistent commitment the school has made to oppose discrimination.

Though recognizing the importance of eradicating discrimination, the district court minimized the state interest in doing so in the present context. The court noted that fraternities and sororities have long existed as single-sex institutions, and that federal anti-discrimination laws specifically exempt fraternities and sororities from their reach. It attached considerable importance to the fact that there "is no law deeming single-sex organizations per se unconstitutional or against national policy." The district court concluded that while eliminating sex discrimination *in general* is a compelling state interest, preventing fraternities from discriminating is not.

The fact that a practice is lawful does not mean that a state may not have a substantial interest in opposing it. An interest need not be protected by federal statutes before it can be considered compelling. In *Roberts*, for instance, the Supreme Court found that Minnesota's public accommodations law served a compelling interest —eradicating discrimination in private clubs—even though the law went further than federal anti-discrimination laws. The state's interest in prohibiting sex discrimination is no less compelling because federal anti-discrimination statutes exempt fraternities.

Moreover, CSI has a substantial interest in making sure that its resources are available to all its students. When a student group is officially recognized by CSI, it becomes entitled to a range of benefits, including use of CSI facilities and services, eligibility for insurance through the school, the right to use the CSI name in conjunction with the group, and the opportunity to apply for funding from the student government. These benefits are funded in part by tuition paid by CSI's students; CSI's non-discrimination policy ensures that all its students have access to the organizations that enjoy these benefits. . . .

In sum, the Fraternity's interests in intimate association are relatively weak; CSI's non-discrimination policy imposes no great burden on the plaintiffs' enjoyment of those interests; the policy serves several important state interests; and the policy is well tailored to effectuate those interests. Given this balance of the pertinent factors, we believe the district court erred in granting a preliminary injunction barring CSI from enforcing its policy of denial of recognition to a group that categorically excludes members on the basis of gender.

> "Disapproval of a tenet of an
> organization's expression does not
> justify the State's effort to compel the
> organization to accept members."

Freedom of Expressive Association Allows Groups to Exclude Members

The Supreme Court's Decision

William Rehnquist

In the following viewpoint William Rehnquist, writing for the majority of the US Supreme Court, argues that the First Amendment right to freedom of expressive association allows groups to exclude members based on their homosexuality when homosexuality is against the group's values. In reviewing the retraction of a homosexual assistant scoutmaster's membership by the Boy Scouts of America, Rehnquist contends that the First Amendment protection of groups may not be limited because of disapproval of the group's views and that it is the right of associations to accept or reject members. Rehnquist was appointed to the US Supreme Court by President Richard Nixon in 1972 and became chief justice in 1986, serving in this role until his retirement in 2005.

William Rehnquist, Majority opinion, *Boy Scouts of America v. Dale*, US Supreme Court, v. 530, June 28, 2000. www.law.cornell.edu. Copyright © 2000 by Legal Information Institute. All rights reserved. Reproduced by permission.

Petitioners are the Boy Scouts of America and the Monmouth Council, a division of the Boy Scouts of America (collectively, Boy Scouts). The Boy Scouts is a private, not-for-profit organization engaged in instilling its system of values in young people. The Boy Scouts asserts that homosexual conduct is inconsistent with the values it seeks to instill. Respondent is James Dale, a former Eagle Scout whose adult membership in the Boy Scouts was revoked when the Boy Scouts learned that he is an avowed homosexual and gay rights activist. The New Jersey Supreme Court held that New Jersey's public accommodations law requires that the Boy Scouts admit Dale. This case presents the question whether applying New Jersey's public accommodations law in this way violates the Boy Scouts' First Amendment right of expressive association. We hold that it does.

Dale's Boy Scout Membership

James Dale entered scouting in 1978 at the age of eight by joining Monmouth Council's Cub Scout Pack 142. Dale became a Boy Scout in 1981 and remained a Scout until he turned 18. By all accounts, Dale was an exemplary Scout. In 1988, he achieved the rank of Eagle Scout, one of Scouting's highest honors.

Dale applied for adult membership in the Boy Scouts in 1989. The Boy Scouts approved his application for the position of assistant scoutmaster of Troop 73. Around the same time, Dale left home to attend Rutgers University. After arriving at Rutgers, Dale first acknowledged to himself and others that he is gay. He quickly became involved with, and eventually became the co-president of, the Rutgers University Lesbian/Gay Alliance. In 1990, Dale attended a seminar addressing the psychological and health needs of lesbian and gay teenagers. A newspaper covering the event interviewed Dale about his advocacy of homosexual teenagers' need for gay role models. In early July 1990, the newspaper published the interview and Dale's photograph over a caption identifying him as the co-president of the Lesbian/Gay Alliance.

Later that month, Dale received a letter from Monmouth Council Executive James Kay revoking his adult membership. Dale wrote to Kay requesting the reason for Monmouth Council's decision. Kay responded by letter that the Boy Scouts "specifically forbid membership to homosexuals." . . .

The Freedom of Expressive Association

In *Roberts v. United States Jaycees* (1984), we observed that "implicit in the right to engage in activities protected by the First Amendment" is "a corresponding right to associate with others in pursuit of a wide variety of political, social, economic, educational, religious, and cultural ends." This right is crucial in preventing the majority from imposing its views on groups that would rather express other, perhaps unpopular, ideas. Government actions that may unconstitutionally burden this freedom may take many forms, one of which is "intrusion into the internal structure or affairs of an association" like a "regulation that forces the group to accept members it does not desire." Forcing a group to accept certain members may impair the ability of the group to express those views, and only those views, that it intends to express. Thus, "[f]reedom of association . . . plainly presupposes a freedom not to associate."

The forced inclusion of an unwanted person in a group infringes the group's freedom of expressive association if the presence of that person affects in a significant way the group's ability to advocate public or private viewpoints. But the freedom of expressive association, like many freedoms, is not absolute. We have held that the freedom could be overridden "by regulations adopted to serve compelling state interests, unrelated to the suppression of ideas, [which] cannot be achieved through means significantly less restrictive of associational freedoms."

To determine whether a group is protected by the First Amendment's expressive associational right, we must determine whether the group engages in "expressive association." The

First Amendment's protection of expressive association is not reserved for advocacy groups. But to come within its ambit, a group must engage in some form of expression, whether it [is] public or private.

The Mission of the Boy Scouts

Because this is a First Amendment case where the ultimate conclusions of law are virtually inseparable from findings of fact, we are obligated to independently review the factual record to ensure that the state court's judgment does not unlawfully intrude on free expression. The record reveals the following. The Boy Scouts is a private, nonprofit organization. According to its mission statement:

> It is the mission of the Boy Scouts of America to serve others by helping to instill values in young people and, in other ways, to prepare them to make ethical choices over their lifetime in achieving their full potential.

> The values we strive to instill are based on those found in the Scout Oath and Law:

> SCOUT OATH
> On my honor I will do my best
> To do my duty to God and my country
> and to obey the Scout Law;
> To help other people at all times;
> To keep myself physically strong,
> mentally awake, and morally straight.

> SCOUT LAW
> A Scout is:
> Trustworthy   Obedient
> Loyal   Cheerful
> Helpful   Thrifty
> Friendly   Brave
> Courteous   Clean
> Kind   Reverent

Former Eagle Scout James Dale speaks with the press outside the Supreme Court during hearings on the constitutional right of the Boy Scouts to exclude gay members. © Alex Wong/ Getty Images.

Thus, the general mission of the Boy Scouts is clear: "[T]o instill values in young people." The Boy Scouts seeks to instill these values by having its adult leaders spend time with the youth members, instructing and engaging them in activities like camping, archery, and fishing. During the time spent with

It's my knot badge. © Used with permission of Signe Wilkinson, the Washington Post Writers Group, and the Cartoonist Group. All rights reserved.

the youth members, the scoutmasters and assistant scoutmasters inculcate them with the Boy Scouts' values—both expressly and by example. It seems indisputable that an association that seeks to transmit such a system of values engages in expressive activity.

Given that the Boy Scouts engages in expressive activity, we must determine whether the forced inclusion of Dale as an assistant scoutmaster would significantly affect the Boy Scouts' ability to advocate public or private viewpoints. This inquiry necessarily requires us first to explore, to a limited extent, the nature of the Boy Scouts' view of homosexuality.

The Boy Scouts' View of Homosexuality

The values the Boy Scouts seeks to instill are "based on" those listed in the Scout Oath and Law. The Boy Scouts explains that the Scout Oath and Law provide "a positive moral code for living; they are a list of 'do's' rather than 'don'ts.'" The Boy Scouts asserts that homosexual conduct is inconsistent with the values embodied in the Scout Oath and Law, particularly with the values represented by the terms "morally straight" and "clean."

Obviously, the Scout Oath and Law do not expressly mention sexuality or sexual orientation. And the terms "morally straight" and "clean" are by no means self-defining. Different people would attribute to those terms very different meanings. For example, some people may believe that engaging in homosexual conduct is not at odds with being "morally straight" and "clean." And others may believe that engaging in homosexual conduct is contrary to being "morally straight" and "clean." The Boy Scouts says it falls within the latter category.

The New Jersey Supreme Court analyzed the Boy Scouts' beliefs and found that the "exclusion of members solely on the basis of their sexual orientation is inconsistent with Boy Scouts' commitment to a diverse and 'representative' membership . . . [and] contradicts Boy Scouts' overarching objective to reach 'all eligible youth.'" The court concluded that the exclusion of members like Dale "appears antithetical to the organization's goals and philosophy." But our cases reject this sort of inquiry; it is not the role of the courts to reject a group's expressed values because they disagree with those values or find them internally inconsistent.

The Boy Scouts asserts that it "teach[es] that homosexual conduct is not morally straight," and that it does "not want to promote homosexual conduct as a legitimate form of behavior." We accept the Boy Scouts assertion. We need not inquire further to determine the nature of the Boy Scouts' expression with respect to homosexuality. . . .

The Boy Scouts publicly expressed its views with respect to homosexual conduct by its assertions in prior litigation. For example, throughout a California case with similar facts filed in the early 1980's, the Boy Scouts consistently asserted the same position with respect to homosexuality that it asserts today. We cannot doubt that the Boy Scouts sincerely holds this view.

An Association's Point of View

We must then determine whether Dale's presence as an assistant scoutmaster would significantly burden the Boy Scouts' desire to not "promote homosexual conduct as a legitimate form of behavior." As we give deference to an association's assertions regarding the nature of its expression, we must also give deference to an association's view of what would impair its expression. That is not to say that an expressive association can erect a shield against anti-discrimination laws simply by asserting that mere acceptance of a member from a particular group would impair its message. But here Dale, by his own admission, is one of a group of gay Scouts who have "become leaders in their community and are open and honest about their sexual orientation." Dale was the co-president of a gay and lesbian organization at college and remains a gay rights activist. Dale's presence in the Boy Scouts would, at the very least, force the organization to send a message, both to the youth members and the world, that the Boy Scouts accepts homosexual conduct as a legitimate form of behavior.

Hurley [v. *Irish American Gay, Lesbian and Bisexual Group of Boston, Inc.* (1995)] is illustrative on this point. There we considered whether the application of Massachusetts' public accommodations law to require the organizers of a private St. Patrick's Day parade to include among the marchers an Irish-American gay, lesbian, and bisexual group, GLIB, violated the parade organizers' First Amendment rights. We noted that the parade organizers did not wish to exclude the GLIB members because of their sexual orientations, but because they wanted to march behind a GLIB banner. We observed:

> [A] contingent marching behind the organization's banner would at least bear witness to the fact that some Irish are gay, lesbian, or bisexual, and the presence of the organized marchers would suggest their view that people of their sexual orientations have as much claim to unqualified social acceptance as heterosexuals. . . . The parade's organizers may not believe

these facts about Irish sexuality to be so, or they may object to unqualified social acceptance of gays and lesbians or have some other reason for wishing to keep GLIB's message out of the parade. But whatever the reason, it boils down to the choice of a speaker not to propound a particular point of view, and that choice is presumed to lie beyond the government's power to control.

Here, we have found that the Boy Scouts believes that homosexual conduct is inconsistent with the values it seeks to instill in its youth members; it will not "promote homosexual conduct as a legitimate form of behavior." As the presence of GLIB in Boston's St. Patrick's Day parade would have interfered with the parade organizers' choice not to propound a particular point of view, the presence of Dale as an assistant scoutmaster would just as surely interfere with the Boy Scout's choice not to propound a point of view contrary to its beliefs.

First Amendment Protection

The New Jersey Supreme Court determined that the Boy Scouts' ability to disseminate its message was not significantly affected by the forced inclusion of Dale as an assistant scoutmaster because of the following findings:

> Boy Scout members do not associate for the purpose of disseminating the belief that homosexuality is immoral; Boy Scouts discourages its leaders from disseminating *any* views on sexual issues; and Boy Scouts includes sponsors and members who subscribe to different views in respect of homosexuality.

We disagree with the New Jersey Supreme Court's conclusion drawn from these findings.

First, associations do not have to associate for the "purpose" of disseminating a certain message in order to be entitled to the protections of the First Amendment. An association must merely engage in expressive activity that could be impaired in order to be entitled to protection. For example, the purpose of the St. Patrick's Day parade in *Hurley* was not to espouse any views about sexual orientation, but we held that the parade organizers had a right to exclude certain participants nonetheless.

Second, even if the Boy Scouts discourages Scout leaders from disseminating views on sexual issues—a fact that the Boy Scouts disputes with contrary evidence—the First Amendment protects the Boy Scouts' method of expression. If the Boy Scouts wishes Scout leaders to avoid questions of sexuality and teach only by example, this fact does not negate the sincerity of its belief discussed above.

Third, the First Amendment simply does not require that every member of a group agree on every issue in order for the group's policy to be "expressive association." The Boy Scouts takes an official position with respect to homosexual conduct, and that is sufficient for First Amendment purposes. In this same vein, Dale makes much of the claim that the Boy Scouts does not revoke the membership of heterosexual Scout leaders that openly disagree with the Boy Scouts' policy on sexual orientation. But if this is true, it is irrelevant. The presence of an avowed homosexual and gay rights activist in an assistant scoutmaster's uniform sends a distinctly different message from the presence of a heterosexual assistant scoutmaster who is on record as disagreeing with Boy Scouts policy. The Boy Scouts has a First Amendment right to choose to send one message but not the other. The fact that the organization does not trumpet its views from the housetops, or that it tolerates dissent within its ranks, does not mean that its views receive no First Amendment protection. . . .

We are not, as we must not be, guided by our views of whether the Boy Scouts' teachings with respect to homosexual conduct are right or wrong; public or judicial disapproval of a tenet of an organization's expression does not justify the State's effort to compel the organization to accept members where such acceptance would derogate from the organization's expressive message. "While the law is free to promote all sorts of conduct in place of harmful behavior, it is not free to interfere with speech for no better reason than promoting an approved message or discouraging a disfavored one, however enlightened either purpose may strike the government" [*Hurley*].

> *"For me, the most important thing*
> *is educating the public about*
> *discrimination at a time when the most*
> *American institution in this country*
> *can say they're anti-gay."*

The Scoutmaster in *Dale* Speaks Out About His Loss at the Supreme Court

Personal Narrative

James Dale, Interviewed by Kera Bolonik

In the following viewpoint Kera Bolonik interviews James Dale, the scoutmaster who took the Boy Scouts of America to court after they revoked his membership for being a homosexual. Dale recounts his experience with the Boy Scouts, his experience bringing a lawsuit against the Boy Scouts, and how he feels about the future. Dale contends that he still believes that he suffered wrongful discrimination even though he ultimately lost the case in the Supreme Court in Boy Scouts of America v. Dale *(2000). Dale claims that the fact that the case got the nation talking about discrimination against homosexuals is part of the battle, as he sees it, in the fight against discrimination. Bolonik is an assistant editor at* New York *magazine.*

On June 28, the U.S. Supreme Court voted 5-4 in favor of the Boy Scouts of America having the constitutional right to exclude gay people. Chief Justice William H. Rehnquist interpreted the First Amendment's protection of the freedom of association to mean that the Supreme Court could not force one of America's most treasured institutions "to accept members where such acceptance would derogate from the organization's expressive message," thus overturning last year's New Jersey Supreme Court ruling that the Scouts had violated the state law banning anti-gay discrimination.

The Dale of *Boy Scouts of America vs. Dale* is a 30-year-old advertising director of *POZ* magazine and a one-time assistant scoutmaster of the Boy Scouts. I befriended James Dale in 1988 during our freshman year at Rutgers, where we were both drawn to the State University of New Jersey for more than just the classes. With its liberal reputation, and proximity to New York City, Rutgers promised to be a comfortable environment for people like us to come out.

But several months after Dale appeared in the pages of Newark's *Star-Ledger* as one of the most visible members of the university's Gay and Lesbian Alliance in 1990, he received two letters—one from the Monmouth Council of Boy Scouts, the other from the district council—informing him that "avowed homosexuals" were not permitted in the organization, and that his 12-year membership was being revoked.

The Boy Scouts taught Dale how to become a leader. Ironically, everything he learned from scouting prepared him for the fight of his life: To defend himself against the group's discriminatory policy. What began as a personal battle of a young man trying to regain his membership with the institution that defined his childhood experience has evolved over a decade into a national issue about the future of gay youth in America—and Dale has become their most vigorous advocate.

A week after the decision was handed down, Dale and I got together for lunch. While the man sitting across from me may not

The author of this viewpoint, Kera Bolonik, attends a book signing of The L Word: Welcome to Our Planet *in New York City.* © Scott Wintrow/Getty Images.

have been victorious in the Supreme Court, I couldn't help but feel that his success in engaging the nation in a crucial discussion about sexual orientation and discrimination had allowed him to emerge a winner.

Kera Bolonik: You've spent your entire adult life fighting for your right to remain a Scout. How did you respond to the Supreme Court decision?

James Dale: On some level I'm just happy to have a level of closure. It's very easy for me to see how the past 10 years were framed by the struggle for gay and lesbian civil equality. There has been an incredible amount of progress, and the 5-4 loss in the Supreme Court shows how far we've gone. But there's still one vote, and it is a very powerful vote. We still have a ways to go.

I had prepared myself on some level that the decision could go either way, but I honestly didn't think we would lose because I believe just as much 10 years ago as I did on June 28, as I do today, that I'm right. Nobody has shaken that conviction. But it was a hard pill to swallow. If I could do it all over again, I would do it exactly the same way. My lawyer, Evan Wolfson from Lambda Legal Defense, has argued an incredible case, and I don't think any other attorney could have gotten that one other vote.

The dissenting opinion was so strong and now Americans can't think of the Boy Scouts of America without thinking of the issue of homosexuality. The Boy Scouts have forever tarnished their image with this case. Granted, I would have loved to be the victor in this case, but in the end, the only thing you're really going to remember is that they are the losers in all of this.

Is there anything more you can do?

I'm definitely going to support people's efforts because I think it is an important fight. What I find really important is that this case highlighted gay youth. When I was a gay kid growing up in suburban New Jersey, the Boy Scouts made me feel good about myself. They taught me to have self-respect and how to be a leader. The light should now shine on how America is dealing with gay youth, and what resources are there for them.

Now that the Boy Scouts have turned their back on gay kids, there has to be some other way to pick up the slack. Let's face it:

I'm an adult. It was a defeat, but I'll survive. I'm more concerned about the kids in the program, where we're going as a community and where gay youth fit into that picture.

The Girl Scouts don't have an anti-gay policy, and filed a brief with the Supreme Court on your behalf. Does that give you hope? Or does that just make you more frustrated with the Boy Scouts?

The Boy Scouts were founded in England roughly 100 years ago, and England dropped their policy of banning gays about four or five years ago to make themselves relevant to the next generation of youth. The Boy Scouts of America have made a foothold in bigotry and discrimination and they are really rendering themselves obsolete for today's youth. That's a sad thing because there was so much potential there.

I see letters to the editors in papers across this country, having conversations about sexual orientation, and it is that conversation that is really the key, so I'm not totally disheartened because I believe as long as that conversation is still taking place, there will be less room for discrimination.

Kids today are coming out, and reading about gay issues in the newspapers. That really wasn't something that I had when I was growing up. As a teenager, I was looking for role models, for messages about what it means to be gay, and really the only thing I found in the '80s was a community responding to HIV and AIDS. Now, hopefully there are other ways that kids can find community and support.

There were definitely no role models for us when we were growing up in the 1980s. For girls, there were gym teachers.

And for men, there were English teachers and drama club. We didn't know where to find role models outside of that. What made it really easy for me to come out in college was learning about the gay community in New York, San Francisco, New Hope, Penn. I think now it's a little easier to learn about gay life because of the Internet.

When you got those letters from the Monmouth Council of Boy Scouts and the district council 10 years ago, did you sense that this was going to evolve into a campaign of this magnitude?

I never thought the Boy Scouts were going to rally around me with rainbow flags in hand and advocate a homosexuality merit badge. But I, of course, didn't expect their reaction, because I didn't know about this policy. That's really the basis of the entire lawsuit. I was a member of this program for 12 years and got many of the awards and honors from the program, and I taught other kids about the fine parts of this program as an assistant scoutmaster. I should have been passing along this anti-gay mission, but I didn't because it wasn't there.

If you had known that an explicit anti-gay policy existed, and the Boy Scouts were as important to you as they were, would it have impacted your gay activism in college?

Had my parents known there was this policy, they would never have me be in an organization that discriminates against a group of people, be they Jews or blacks or gays. The thing about scouting, though, is that you're taught to be active, to be a leader. In relation to gay life, everyone likes to call an openly gay person an activist.

You were the president of the university's Lesbian Gay Association, making you the spokesperson for gay activities and politics on campus at the time, though.

Yes. That letter from the Boy Scouts probably made me more of an activist. When I was discriminated against, it motivated me to be more out there, and more political about gay and lesbian issues. But I do kind of cringe at the whole label of activist because that has been used against me in the Supreme Court. I get: "James Dale is an activist. He's not a person, he's a symbol." If you're an activist, they don't need you.

During my first year in college, I was unconsciously building myself a nest of support so that when I did eventually come out, nobody would have a hard time with it. There really wasn't a lot of discrimination against me at Rutgers until this happened with the Boy Scouts.

Did you feel personally hurt by the Boy Scouts reaction to your coming out?

Yeah. I mean, the letter was signed by somebody I knew. It was *the* thing that I did when I was younger. To have them suddenly say, "you're gay, you're out," was painful.

But I also expected the whole thing to play out, "I'm right, they're wrong." The Boy Scouts have their own fair review process. There were three hearings, and though they said I could come to all three of them, they didn't invite me. It wasn't fair play. I went to Lambda Legal Defense right away, though when my case started, there was no Gay Rights Law in New Jersey, so it wasn't a very strong case.

Did you bide your time until there was?

No, because nobody knew that the law was going to pass. But when the law got passed in 1992, I suddenly went from having no case to a very strong case, and mine was the first under the Gay Rights Law in New Jersey.

How has this impacted your personal life over the last 10 years? Has your family been supportive?

It led my family to become advocates for gay and lesbian civil rights. When this case started, my brother wasn't out yet. He is four years older than me, and came out when he was 28.

But for me, within a matter of months of coming out to my parents, I was suing the Boy Scouts. My parents were with me at the Supreme Court. They talked to newspapers about the decision. They've been really, really wonderful about it. This whole thing has really shown what family values are all about: Taking care of your children, standing by them, being involved in their lives. My parents were not gay advocates when I was a kid. My father was in the military. When I came out to them, I got the traditional fighting from my father and crying from my mother.

It has been hard, emotionally, to appear before the country as one-dimensional. To be defined as gay is just one little piece of who I am. When I was younger, it seemed like a bigger piece, but I am a fully realized person with many different interests, and this is only one facet of who I am. Being the "Gay Boy Scout" is not the easiest label to live with for a decade. It's also weird being in the media. This public thing intersects with your private life, and it's hard to keep your life in check and in balance. When the case requires attention, it takes it.

Did you feel emotionally equipped to handle everything that comes with suing a major American institution?

Yes, for the most part. But I think if somebody said to me what this was going to be 10 years ago, it would have been very overwhelming. It has been very stressful for some of my relationships, and I also think it probably helped others. I mean, it's a part of who I am, though I think it is always weird to meet somebody who knows something public about you. It's like getting to know somebody in reverse. That's not always the easiest thing.

You and your lawyer have been a veritable two-man army. Has this made you feel like you were all alone in this? Who has been there for you?

People have submitted affidavits, and lawyers have been working around the clock filing briefs and motions. Often there are more people that have been involved with this case than I even know about. I am so indebted to so many different people. The people across the country that write letters to the editor, and the columnists that write editorials demonstrate to me that America gets it. When there's a human being discriminated against, people understand that.

There are times, though, that I have felt lonely, wondering who out there will understand this type of thing or the different pressures involved with it. I think one of the hardest things that I found is the people who offer their support, and you find you don't know what to say to them. You, or the case, means something to somebody, and you don't know how to be that something for them.

If your case had won in the Supreme Court, what would that have meant to you? Was it an issue of principle for you? Or had you really wanted to be a lifelong member of the Scouts?

It wasn't just principle. I mean, on the one hand it is. The fairest way to answer this is that I want to have a kid, and if it is a "he" and he wanted to be a Boy Scout, I would've loved to have been a part of that with him. But I wouldn't want my kid in the Scouts now because the Supreme Court has given them a license to be a small-minded organization.

With my case, it's very easy for the Boy Scouts to say, oh, he's the only one, he's the activist. But there are tons of kids who were thrown out. And it's the kids who don't have the resources or the support, and they're the ones that need it the most.

What lies ahead for you?

I'm always going to be committed to the things I believe in. I can't walk away from these issues. I would hope what I've done has motivated people to get involved, and make change. I feel like I've done my part, seeing something through from beginning, middle to completion.

I don't want to go on being the "Gay Boy Scout" for the rest of my life. Other people are very able, and the work on this issue has only just begun. For me, the most important thing is educating the public about discrimination at a time when the most American institution in this country can say they're anti-gay. It calls into question what it means to be American. The Supreme Court has essentially said, you are the anti-gay Boy Scouts of America, so now they have to live with that.

As for me, I am looking forward to getting on with the rest of my life. I am ready for a change. I have no idea what I'm going to do next, and I am very excited about that fact.

> *"As with freedom of speech, true freedom of association means that some people will choose to exercise the right in a way that doesn't find favor with the majority."*

Freedom of Association Should Not Be Limited to Avoid Discrimination

Selwyn Duke

In the following viewpoint Selwyn Duke argues that freedom of association in the United States has been almost entirely eliminated. Duke contends that the attempt to rid private businesses of discrimination has resulted in the elimination of freedom of association. Duke believes private businesses should be allowed to discriminate as a right of freedom of association and argues that social pressure will take care of any egregious discrimination. The alternative, Duke concludes, is a regulation of association that rests on the current popular prejudices of the majority. Duke is a columnist and public speaker.

Howard Weyers, President of Weyco Corporation, is worried about his employees' health and his company's health insurance premiums. So worried, in fact, that he has instituted a policy mandating that his employees may not puff on the vilest of vile weeds—tobacco—even at home. The policy would compel employees to submit to random testing, and if a hapless individual happened to register positive for nicotine, he would be terminated posthaste.

Contradictions About Discrimination

Ahh, paternalistic puppeteering at its best. Of course, though, we all know that smoking is deleterious to one's health and health insurance costs have skyrocketed. And why should we as a society have to subsidize those who choose to engage in irresponsible behaviors? Besides, in Otto von Bismarck, iron-fist-inside-a-velvet-glove fashion, Weyco is providing some fatherly guidance to complement its fatherly strictures, in the form of wellness counseling, subsidies for health club memberships and company-paid smoking-cessation classes. And doesn't such self-destructive behavior, coupled with the imperatives of being your brother's keeper and holding down health insurance costs, provide reason enough for such a prohibition? Okay, I think I'm finally getting it.

Now, learning is exciting, so I think I'll test my grasp of this principle by applying it to an analogous situation. Here's a good one: we know that practicing homosexuals also engage in high-risk behaviors, as borne out by a study showing that their average lifespan is forty-two. Thus, in keeping with the aforementioned principle, I'm sure that no one would mind if employers applied the same standard to everyone and fired homosexuals who refused to cease their high-risk, health-costs-raising behavior. Insensitive, say you? Hey, it's not as if we would just cast them to the winds—we'd offer them free classes in controlling their sexual impulses.

What do I hear? 'Can you say Equal Employment Opportunity Commission,' 'lawsuit' and 'discrimination'? I see, hmm, so then public health and its attendant costs are not the overriding concerns, since they are trumped by the imperative of eliminating discrimination. But wait, if the latter is the overriding concern, then why allow such discrimination against smokers? Ah, the contradictions that abound in societies in which emotions carry the day.

The Freedom of Association

Truth be known, I support Mr. Weyers' right to discriminate in his hiring practices. But I'm not going to posture about how much it pains me to see people destroying themselves, nor will I shed a tear for a system that finds itself strained because it places the burdens of some groups' bad decisions on others. No, I support his right for what is both the least mentioned and only valid reason to do so: freedom of association.

Freedom of association is implied in our Constitution, and in no substantial measure can we consider ourselves a free people without it. Yet, the principle is rarely thought about, hardly mentioned and almost universally ignored. What it would guarantee us is obvious: the right to associate as we see fit in our private dealings.

And there's the rub: as with freedom of speech, true freedom of association means that some people will choose to exercise the right in a way that doesn't find favor with the majority. So yes, it certainly would afford Mr. Weyer the right to exclude smokers, but it also means that employers would have a right to refuse to hire homosexuals, heterosexuals, whites, blacks, men, women, Catholics, Muslims, guys named Selwyn, or any other group that found disfavor with them.

Unlike freedom of speech, however, freedom of association has been trampled to a point where it's non-existent in the private business sector. What happened was that a few decades ago an activist Supreme Court declared private businesses to be 'public accommodations' and on that basis stripped millions of business owners of their freedom of association. Of course, those who support such anti-discrimination laws believe that theirs is the moral position, so let's examine the morality of the matter.

The Private Sector

A man's home is his castle, and I think you'll agree that I can include in—or exclude from my abode whomever I want. For instance, if I refused all atheists entry, while I suspect that some of you would have contempt for my decision, I also think you'd say that I was well within my rights to do so. After all, it's my home, paid for with my money. Okay, then, pray tell, why should I lose that right simply because I decide to erect a few more tables and start selling food?

The truth is that I shouldn't be robbed of that right. Moreover, for the government to dictate to a private business owner what policies must prevail within his own business, paid for with his own money and created by the sweat of his own brow, is nothing less than the brand of immorality called tyranny.

I know what you're thinking: how can we allow people to discriminate on the basis of race, sex or religion, some of the most invidious ways imaginable? Well, the first thing we have to realize is that, as with freedom of speech, freedom of association means nothing unless it protects the most odious forms of the exercise of the freedom. After all, of what value is it if it's only applied to popular forms? The majority will almost never seek to suppress that which is popular. Consequently, if such a 'freedom' is only applicable when the behavior is popular, it has lost its raison d'être [reason for existence]. Popular behavior's popularity is protection enough.

This is why I said that freedom of association is non-existent in the private business sector. For, if all we will say is that one can associate in any way that falls within the bounds of the popular, it's tantamount to saying that we have no freedom of association whatsoever.

The Pressure to Conform

And then there's the law of unintended consequences. Did you ever wonder why the Boy Scouts and other traditional organizations are attacked with lawsuit after lawsuit, all on the basis

Freedom of Association and Choice

> How a person uses the right to associate (which necessarily means the right not to associate) is a matter of individual choice profoundly influenced by the cultural context. That a person has the right to make these choices on his or her own cannot be denied by anyone who believes in liberty.
>
> *Llewellyn H. Rockwell Jr., "Freedom of Association," Mises Daily, June 3, 2010.*

of discrimination complaints? There was the atheist who sued the Scouts because they had God in their pledge; there was the girl who sued because they only allow boys, and the homosexual who sued because they won't allow openly homosexual leaders. Wonder no more; it's because a long, long time ago in a galaxy right here, we allowed a precedent to be set stating that the government could dictate to private entities what membership, employment, and patronage policies they must embrace. And Hell followed with it.

It's truly the ultimate in statist foolishness. In the name of preventing a minuscule percentage of the population from discriminating in egregious ways, we have placed Big Brother's shackles on everyone. A more sane approach at this point in time would be to rely on social pressure to bring invidious discriminators to heel. After all, most anyone who would engage in overt discrimination of a truly immoral sort would have to endure the scorn, ostracism and reduction in patronage that would result.

Then there's the irony that the tramplers of freedom of association limit diversity despite purporting to be its staunchest advocates. For one small example, let's go back to the smoking

The author argues that giving special dispensation from anti-discrimination laws to women-only health clubs contradicts the principles of freedom of association. © Michelangelo Gratton/ Getty Images.

issue. Were it not for New York City's smoking ban, you would find restaurants that allowed smoking, those that didn't and those that tried to satisfy both needs. For this is what the market does: it responds to collective needs and desires. Now, however, all we have are non-smoking restaurants. Add to that the elimination of many single-sex schools, clubs and whatever else the diversity-police find anathema, and you have the makings of a monochrome society.

It's a bit like insisting that every can of paint contain equal amounts of every color, so as to ensure that every color has a place in every can. This certainly would increase the constituent elements in every can, but the end result is that you would be left with only one color of paint in the world. Trying to make the constitution of every unit of society uniformly diverse does not yield true diversity, for it serves to make every unit the same.

The Tyranny of Prejudices

This is why important principles like freedom of association must be respected. But as far as these issues go, respected principles are in very short supply. At times the social-engineers will say that a policy designed to enhance health cannot be implemented because it's discriminatory, but at other times will advocate a discriminatory policy because it enhances public health. On the one hand they will complain about men-only membership policies at places like Augusta National Golf Club, but on the other will offer a special dispensation from anti-discrimination laws to placate the proponents of women-only health clubs.

Why the contradiction? It's because the people in question are not governed by principle, but prejudice. Neither rooting out discrimination nor the imperative of protecting public health is an unassailable guiding light, for either one may be cast aside in a given instance if adherence to it would yield a politically-incorrect result. And freedom of association isn't even a consideration. The truth is that the social-engineers—the ones who lurk on college campuses, hide black hearts under black robes or practice the fine art of demagoguery in our hollowed hells of government— want to set themselves up as arbiters of what kind of prejudice is palatable, using their own prejudices as a yardstick.

And the prejudices are like the stars in the sky. Smoking is no longer trendy, but homosexuality is; the Boy Scouts are out in San Francisco, but a law prohibiting smoking in private establishments and even outdoor public places is in [I wonder, did it ever occur to the lunkheads who conjured up this little taste of totalitarianism that motor vehicles create infinitely more pollution than smokers do?]. Christianity in schools is out, but left-wing indoctrination is in. And what group will be persecuted next week, next month or next year? In Europe, the Ladies Golf Tour is being forced to allow the participation of a transsexual by the European Union anti-discrimination Nazis. Don't think that we could never be subject to such insane government dictation, and that the casualty won't be your church, club or some organization close to your heart. With the freedom of association already relegated to the dustbin of history, such tyranny is only a few bad Supreme Court appointments away.

Organizations to Contact

The editors have compiled the following list of organizations concerned with the issues debated in this book. The descriptions are derived from materials provided by the organizations.

Alliance Defense Fund (ADF)

15100 N. 90th Street, Scottsdale, AZ 85260
(480) 444-0020 • fax (480) 444-0028
website: www.alliancedefensefund.org

ADF is a Christian organization that works to defend religious freedom. ADF provides legal defense for cases involving religious freedom and the sanctity of life, marriage, and family. ADF publishes several books, brochures, and pamphlets, including, "The Truth About Student Rights."

American Center for Law and Justice (ACLJ)

PO Box 90555, Washington, DC 20090-0555
(800) 296-4529
website: www.aclj.org

ACLJ is dedicated to protecting religious and constitutional freedoms. ACLJ has participated in numerous cases before the Supreme Court, Federal Court of Appeals, Federal District Courts, and various state courts regarding freedom of religion and freedom of speech. ACLJ has numerous memos and position papers available on its website, including, "Protecting the Rights of Students."

American Civil Liberties Union (ACLU)

125 Broad Street, 18th Floor, New York, NY 10004
(212) 549-2500
e-mail: infoaclu@aclu.org
website: www.aclu.org

The ACLU is a national organization that works to defend Americans' civil rights as guaranteed in the US Constitution. The ACLU works in courts, legislatures, and communities to defend First Amendment rights, the right to equal protection, the right to due process, and the right to privacy. The ACLU publishes the semiannual newsletter *Civil Liberties Alert*, as well as other publications, including "Reclaiming Our Rights: Declaration of First Amendment Rights and Grievances."

American Jewish Congress

115 E. 57th Street, Suite 11, New York, NY 10022
(212) 879-4500 • fax (212) 758-1633
e-mail: contact@ajcongress.org
website: www.ajcongress.org

The American Jewish Congress is an association of Jewish Americans organized to defend Jewish interests at home and abroad. The American Jewish Congress engages in public policy advocacy—using diplomacy, legislation, and the courts—to defend religious freedom in the United States. The American Jewish Congress has several publications available on its website, including, "Religion and the Public Schools: A Summary of the Law."

Center for Campus Free Speech

328 S. Jefferson Avenue, Suite 620, Chicago, IL 60661
(312) 544-4438
e-mail: center@campusspeech.org
website: www.campusspeech.org

The Center for Campus Free Speech was created by students, faculty, administrators, and others to protect and promote free speech on university campuses. The Center acts as a clearinghouse of information, provides specialized support to campuses, and connects concerned educators, administrators, lawyers, and students into a national network. The Center publishes a variety of reports and papers supporting free speech on campus, including, "Speech Codes: Speech Codes and Other Restrictions on the Content of Speech."

Center for Public Education
1680 Duke Street, Alexandria, VA 22314
(703) 838-6722 • fax (703) 548-5613
website: www.centerforpubliceducation.org
e-mail: centerforpubliced@nsba.org

The Center for Public Education is a resource center set up by the National School Boards Association (NSBA). The Center for Public Education works to provide information about public education, leading to more understanding about schools, more community-wide involvement, and better decision-making by school leaders on behalf of all students in their classrooms. Among the many publications available at the Center's website is "Free Speech and Public Schools."

First Amendment Coalition
534 4th Street, Suite B, San Rafael, CA 94901
(415) 460-5060 • fax (415) 460-5155
website: www.firstamendmentcoalition.org

The First Amendment Coalition is a nonprofit public interest organization dedicated to advancing free speech, more open and accountable government, and public participation in civic affairs. The First Amendment Coalition offers free legal consultations, engages in litigation, offers educational programs, and engages in public advocacy. The Coalition's website contains First Amendment news and opinion, as well as a searchable database from its legal hotline information service, Asked & Answered.

Freedom Forum
555 Pennsylvania Avenue NW, Washington, DC 20001
(202) 292-6100

e-mail: news@freedomforum.org
website: www.freedomforum.org

The Freedom Forum is a nonpartisan foundation dedicated to free press, free speech, and free spirit for all people. The forum's First Amendment Center (www.firstamendmentcenter.org) works to preserve and protect First Amendment freedoms through information and education. It publishes the annual report, *State of the First Amendment*, as well as numerous publications, including, *The Silencing of Student Voices*.

National Coalition Against Censorship (NCAC)

275 Seventh Avenue, Suite 1504, New York, NY 10001
(212) 807-6222 • fax (212) 807-6245
e-mail: ncac@ncac.org
website: www.ncac.org

NCAC is an alliance of fifty-two participating organizations dedicated to protecting free expression and access to information. It has many projects dedicated to educating the public and protecting free expression, including the Free Expression Policy Project, the Kids' Right to Read Project, The Knowledge Project: Censorship and Science, and the Youth Free Expression Network. Among its publications is *The First Amendment in Schools*.

National Youth Rights Association (NYRA)

1101 15th Street NW, Suite 200, Washington, DC 20005
(202) 835-1739
website: www.youthrights.org

NYRA is a youth-led nonprofit organization dedicated to fighting for the civil rights and liberties of young people. NYRA works to lower the voting age, lower the drinking age, repeal curfew laws, protect student rights, and fight against ageism. Among NYRA's publications available on its website is "Analysis of US Curfew Laws."

People for the American Way (PFWA)

2000 M Street NW, Suite 400, Washington, DC 20036
(202) 467-4999
website: www.pfaw.org

PFWA is an organization that fights for progressive values: equal rights, freedom of speech, religious liberty, and equal justice under the law for every American. PFWA works to build and nurture communities of support for its values and to equip those communities to promote progressive policies, elect progressive candidates, and hold public officials accountable. Among its publications on the topic of freedom of speech is the report *Back to School with the Religious Right*.

Rutherford Institute

PO Box 7482, Charlottesville, VA 22906-7482
(434) 978-3888 • fax (434) 978-1789
e-mail: staff@rutherford.org
website: www.rutherford.org

The Rutherford Institute is a civil liberties organization. The Rutherford Institute provides legal services in the defense of religious and civil liberties and aims to educate the public on important issues affecting their constitutional freedoms. The Rutherford Institute publishes commentary, articles, and books, including, "The Future Looks Bleak for the First Amendment."

For Further Reading

Books

Floyd Abrams, *Speaking Freely: Trials of the First Amendment.* New York: Penguin Books, 2006.

Kenneth Dautrich, David A. Yalof, and Mark Hugo Lopez, *The Future of the First Amendment: The Digital Media, Civic Education, and Free Expression Rights in America's High Schools.* Lanham, MD: Rowman & Littlefield Publishers, 2008.

Anne Proffitt Dupre, *Speaking Up: The Unintended Costs of Free Speech in Public Schools.* Cambridge, MA: Harvard University Press, 2009.

Stephen M. Feldman, *Free Expression and Democracy in America: A History.* Chicago: University of Chicago Press, 2008.

Charles C. Haynes, Sam Chaltain, and Susan M. Glisson, *First Freedoms: A Documentary History of First Amendment Rights in America.* New York: Oxford University Press, 2006.

Thomas A. Jacobs, *Teens Take It to Court: Young People Who Challenged the Law—and Changed Your Life.* Minneapolis: Free Spirit, 2006.

Anthony Lewis, *Freedom for the Thought That We Hate: A Biography of the First Amendment.* New York: MJF Books, 2011.

Dawn C. Nunziato, *Virtual Freedom: Net Neutrality and Free Speech in the Internet Age.* Stanford, CA: Stanford Law Books, 2009.

Brad O'Leary, *Shut Up, America!: The End of Free Speech.* Los Angeles: WND Books, 2009.

R. Murray Thomas, *God in the Classroom: Religion and America's Public Schools*. Westport, CT: Praeger, 2007.

Lynn S. Urban, *The Deterrent Effects of Curfews: An Evaluation of Juvenile Probationers*. El Paso, TX: LFB Scholarly Publishing, 2007.

Periodicals and Internet Sources

Teresa Ann Boeckel, "Curfew's Mixed Reviews: Some Argue that Daytime Provisions Aren't Necessary Because of Truancy Laws," *McClatchy-Tribune Business News*, April 20, 2008.

Caitlin Carpenter, "For Teens, It's Curfew Time . . . at the Mall," *Christian Science Monitor*, June 6, 2007.

Current Events, "Grounded . . . Every Night? Teens Locked in Debate Over Town Curfews," October 14, 2005.

Danielle Diviaio, "The Government Is Establishing Your Child's Curfew," *St. John's Journal of Legal Commentary*, Spring-Summer 2007.

Frederick M. Hess, "Do Student Rights Interfere with Teaching and Learning in Public Schools?" *CQ Researcher*, June 1, 2009.

Tom Jacobs, "10 Supreme Court Cases Every Teen Should Know: Part 1," *New York Times Upfront*, September 3, 2010.

Tom Jacobs, "10 Supreme Court Cases Every Teen Should Know: Part 2," *New York Times Upfront*, September 17, 2010.

Jeff Jacoby, "The Indispensable Freedom of Association," Townhall.com, April 11, 2011.

Brian Johnson, "Driving While Young: Why the City's Curfew Isn't All That," *Jackson Free Press*, October 12, 2005.

Judy Keen, "Malls' Night Restrictions on Teens Paying Off," *USA Today*, March 15, 2007.

Joseph Kellard, "The Anti-Self-Responsibility Movement," *Capitalism*, August 22, 2004. www.capitalismmagazine.com.

Adam Liptak, "The First Amendment," *New York Times Upfront*, October 9, 2006.

Frank D. LoMonte, "Student Journalism Confronts a New Generation of Legal Challenges," *Human Rights*, Summer 2008.

Martha McCarthy, "Beyond the Wall of Separation: Church-State Concerns in Public Schools," *Phi Delta Kappan*, June 2009.

Sean McCollum, "Mall Curfews: Teen Discrimination?" *Literary Cavalcade*, January 2005.

James McKinney, "Curfews: A New Crime-Fighting Tool," *Time*, September 11, 2008.

Anusha Mohan and Molly Henningsen, "Teen Time Check: Curfews Can Be a Sticking Point Between Parents and Teens," *Contra Costa Times*, February 9, 2006.

Jennifer Morron, "Teen Curfew?" *Gotham Gazette*, March 2006.

Jayne O'Donnell, "Deadly Teen Auto Crashes Show a Pattern," *USA Today*, March 1, 2005.

Betsey Taylor, "Malls Try Teen Curfews to Draw Shoppers," *Washington Post*, April 5, 2007.

George Wilson, "Misplaced Punishment," *Washington Informer*, August 3–9, 2006.

Anthony E. Wolf, "Sorry, You Can't Stop Teenage Snark," *Globe and Mail*, November 25, 2008.

Index